SCOTLAND

Frontispiece:
EDINBURGH
(The Scotsman)

SCOTLAND

By
IAN FINLAY

OXFORD UNIVERSITY PRESS
LONDON . NEW YORK . TORONTO
1945

OXFORD UNIVERSITY PRESS
AMEN HOUSE, E.C.4

London   Edinburgh   Glasgow   New York
Toronto   Melbourne   Capetown   Bombay
Calcutta   Madras

HUMPHREY MILFORD
PUBLISHER TO THE UNIVERSITY

PRINTED IN GREAT BRITAIN
1944 . SB421

PREFACE

THIS little book is to some extent a record of a journey of exploration. It attempts to cover many aspects of the Scotland of to-day, and for the writing of four-fifths of it I can advance no qualification at all beyond a fairly well-established general residential one. I have, however, enjoyed straying boldly into fields little known to me, and I hope some inkling of the enjoyment has found its way into the pages which follow. I wish only to make it clear that the many people who have helped me explore are not necessarily implicated in the conclusions which I have drawn.

Among those many people are Mr. James Fergusson, Dr. Henry W. Meikle, Librarian of the National Library of Scotland, and Mr. William Beattie, Keeper of Printed Books in the same Library. To Mr. W. Henderson Pringle I have turned for advice on many occasions. Dr. F. Fraser Darling has been generous with suggestions on the treatment of the Highland problem. The ready co-operation of the Publishers has been a pleasure at all stages.

Sources of illustrations are acknowledged in their place, but I would mention specially the trouble taken by Mr. Alan Reiach and by Miss Rhoda Spence. I am indebted to Mr. Hew Lorimer for agreeing to the use of his 'St. Andrew', illustrated on Plate X.

I. F.

Edinburgh
  August 1944

CONTENTS

MAPS

ILLUSTRATIONS

TO MY WIFE

CHAPTER I

O N the walls of the great Banqueting Hall of Edinburgh Castle hang many weapons. Among them are trophies of 'Highland' pistols, and on the lock-plate of each pistol the name *Bissell* is stamped. Closely examined, the barrel will be found to have what appears to be a cross punched deep into the metal. This is the Birmingham proof-mark, and Bissell would seem to have been a gunsmith of that city, so that, unlike the magnificent *claidheamh-mor* and targes under the same roof, the pistols are not Highland at all. But oddly enough, they are the most significant objects in the hall. They are symbols of the Celt's defeat in his last bid to defy fate on the mainland of Britain—symbols of the subsequent cleavage of the Highland Gael from the Lowlander, an ethnological, cultural, and economic enormity. The Gael's military defeat was inevitable: Culloden was a mere last rearguard action in a Celtic retreat that lasted from the day the Roman legions crossed the Alps. The splitting of Gael from Lowlander has been a foolish domestic tragedy: a supreme disaster for Scotland, but a disaster also for the united peoples of Britain. Divided against herself, Scotland for two centuries has groped for the identity and unity which she is only now beginning to find.

These pistols are also symbols of a national hoax which helped to mislead the Scots into believing nothing was amiss. The Bissell pistols are mass-produced imitations of the beautiful old silver-inlaid weapons which families of craftsmen for many generations made for the clansmen—weapons which brought to light a wonderful and exciting new blossoming of the ancient Celtic mastery of decorative design. Those fine old weapons had been proscribed after the 'Forty-five; but Pitt, acting on the subtle advice of Duncan Forbes of Culloden, reversed the hated ban on the Highlander's bearing arms. He recruited him into the British Army—and equipped him with those Brummagem imitations of his ancient weapons. The Gael has a childish delight in finery and glitter, and when Pitt

played the Pied Piper up and down the glens not only did he
succeed in drawing off the most enterprising and vigorous of
the clansmen, but he began—with the best of intentions—that
Highland haemophilia which has since drained the best Gaelic
blood to invigorate enterprises in every corner of the world
but its own glens and straths. This weakening of Gaeldom
further emphasized the cleavage between Highlands and
Lowlands. Growing poorer and more backward, the Gael was
looked on at last by the Lowlander as a kind of poor relation,
if indeed a relation at all.

The year 1814 saw the publication of *Waverley* and the
spread of the Romantic Revival. Sir Walter Scott has been
pilloried as the presiding genius of an era the legacy of which
has been Rob Roy melodrama, the bogus baronialism which
began with Abbotsford, and the Trossachs pilgrimage. This
is unjust. Scott had his weaknesses, but he was a very great
man and he did more to restore the prestige of his country
than anyone had done in a century. In spite of Edinburgh's
loss of Court and Parliament, Scott recreated her the capital of
Scotland, and indeed for a few short years the capital of the
English literary world. To purists, much of what he did was
anathema. He had probably little understanding of the Celtic
mind, which is the predominant creative force in Scottish culture. But if there had been others to succeed him with like
vision, patriotism, and personality, Scotland might have begun
to find herself two or three generations sooner than she has
done. Bereft of him, the Romantic Revival lost momentum and
disintegrated into a source of diversion and a tourist attraction
which yet again labelled the Highlander as of a race apart.
Scotland became personified by a wild-eyed, bearded clans-
man, useful as background stuff for historical novels or for the
cover design of 'bus-tour' pamphlets, and the Gael and his
problems were mercilessly falsified to fit in with the sentimental longings of tired townsmen in the south. How such
falsifications can erect barriers to understanding is well seen
to-day in the film-prejudiced conception of the American held
by millions in this country. Yet America is populous, rich,
and powerful, and it is in the interest of her friends to get to
know her better: the misconception will be broken down.
Scotland is neither populous, rich, nor powerful. The false
idea of her is perpetuated every time an Allied soldier buys a

comic Balmoral bonnet as a souvenir or goes home with the idea that the most vital people in Scotland are the ghosts of conspirators who walked four hundred years ago. And many Scots are fully satisfied those are the things their visitors should take away with them. Scotland is not America. To a small people, those misconceptions are deadly mockery when behind the façade of them there are desperate problems in need of understanding and sympathy.

I have begun with this assault upon Romanticism because Romanticism is Scotland's Old Man of the Sea. Scotland, for far too many Scots, has been a kind of Little Grey Home in the West, a place to sing and weep a few pleasant tears over after the day's work is done. This cult of Romanticism has brought about a curious divorce between Scotland and the Scots. It is perhaps the heritage of *laissez-faire* and individualism, but the average Scot instinctively pursues his career to as successful a conclusion as he can achieve without regard to whether this leads him furth of Scotland. The Scots, therefore, as a race—the Scots of England, America, Australasia, and the remotest stations in Africa and the East—have never ceased to flourish; but Scotland has been dying by inches. This single-minded pursuit of a career no matter whether it entails the sacrifice of home and family ties is in certain ways no doubt a virtue in the Scots; but it is a virtue the French, the Germans, the Russians, and almost any other race find it hard to appreciate. Even the English are not so given to practising it as the Scots. Largely perhaps it is due to the troubled times of the past. Attachment to one's country means attachment to little things—to the tankard of ale by the village cricket-pitch, to the sound of bells in a cathedral close. Those things are tokens of security. Scottish life has rarely for long been secure and undisturbed enough to render those gentle bonds between man and his surroundings unbreakable. Lately, and especially since the war, it has been recognized that such bonds must be forged. First the remains of the fickle glue of sentiment and romantic attachment must be scoured away, and Scotland can well do without it. The land, in a favourite phrase of a good friend of mine, 'needs to be loved', not rhapsodized over. The loving of her must not stop at a regretful pang, no matter how sincere, for 'the lone shieling and the misty isle'. The land must be made to feel it in the only way in which land *can* feel—by the work of hands eager to labour in and upon it.

CHAPTER II

THIS splitting of Highlanders and Lowlanders has become necessary in dealing with the Scots, but it should never be forgotten that the distinction is artificial and a convenience. Ethnologically, it is not valid. The Gael of Wester Ross is certainly a very different sort of person from the Border farmer: those are extreme types. But the dividing line is nebulous. The differences between Highlander and Lowlander are largely the result of political, economic, and cultural influences over a thousand years and more. Certainly, one is the purer Celt, the other not so pure. There were centuries of infiltration by Danes and Norsemen, Saxons and Angles and, later, Flemings, all except the Norse by way of the east coast, yet the invaders did not push the original inhabitants into the mountain fastnesses of the north and west. The stock remained stubbornly Celtic, as place-names, customs, institutions and even folk-lore in the Lowlands abundantly prove. Gaelic was the tongue spoken in many parts of the Lowlands until comparatively recent times. Conversely, there is Norse blood in many Highlanders, and some clans—Clan Fraser is an instance—are of Norman origin, although they adopted the ways and customs of the Gael. It is a basic distinction between Scot and Englishman that the Scot in greater or less degree is a Celt.

It is usual to draw the Gael as a melancholy, romantic fellow, always sitting on a rocky shore and dreaming of a splendid but unrecoverable past. The rocky shore is allowable: the Celt's historic retreat was brought up short only by the Atlantic. If he looks back, this is not surprising. But the melancholy is only one of those insidious half-truths which the Romanticists seized upon. . . .

'The grey wind weeps, the grey wind weeps,
  the grey wind weeps:
Dust on her breast, dust on her eyes,
  the grey wind weeps!'

Thus 'Fiona Macleod' and the Celtic Twilight. No one who knows the deserted shielings, etched against the unreal beauty of Ross-shire sea-lochs, with the unbelievable shapes of Quinag or Stac Polly looming through a drapery of cloud piled up against them by a sou'wester off the Minch, can help feeling that those nostalgic verses are in tune with them. They sing of ghosts and emptiness and finality, and try to sanctify those things as beautiful. They imply a gentle *Götterdämmerung* of the Gael. What they never do is to look beyond this Atlantic to the vigorous, multiplying, prosperous communities of Gaels on the far shores. The Gael in America, Australia, New Zealand is of the same stock as the remnant of the race left behind. He is in fact the best strain of the Gael, even more faithful to his origins and customs, and in Canada alone there are said to be more speakers of Gaelic than in the Highlands of Scotland. Of three men of an overseas Canadian contingent recently by chance taken to a *ceilidh* in Glasgow, two understood every word of the proceedings, although their guide understood not one. The Gael has his moods, but, far from being melancholic, he is an ebullient and even a noisy person. He has always loved gay colour and sound. Caesar noted the 'celerity' of the Celt in mind and body, and anyone who has been present at a social gathering of Highlanders where there was music must have noticed the complete absence of that dreary sentimentality in which the Anglo-Saxon habitually soaks himself on such occasions. The Gael, indeed, is perhaps less melancholy than any other race would have been in his circumstances.

He has two traditional loyalties: the land and the clan. Superimposed on them is a still-surviving feudalism.

His land loyalty is not simply a question of a love of the earth and its fruits. It is not the feeling of a frugal Frenchman or Chinese for the soil which supports him. Indeed, Celtic blood seems to carry a certain faint distaste and contempt for lush land, and it is a long time since the Gael has been a farmer. By nature he is a warrior and a herdsman and a hunter, preferring to range over great spaces carelessly rather than to grub methodically and maintain the fruitfulness of a few acres by intensive cultivation. Like other warrior tribesmen, whether in Africa, Asia, or America, he prefers to leave the humdrum labour to his womenfolk. This is as true to-day as ever. Utilization of his water for electric power will have a special appeal if he is convinced it will reduce his need to labour and increase his leisure. This is not intended as irony. What with his delight in conversation and music and hospitality, he retains strongly the instinct—almost lost by more sophisticated communities—for making the proper use of leisure. He still retains a certain sure grasp of the art of living which the Industrial Revolution destroyed in the Lowlands. The late A. G. Macdonell wrote trenchantly about his strutting before the theatrical backcloth of his mountains in everlasting dress-rehearsal, and there was some justice in what he wrote; but at least the Gael creates the drama for himself, when others prefer to accept uncritically what they can get for two-and-sixpence in a cinema. The Highlander's land loyalty, in brief, is pride in the land because it is the ancient home of his race, and the fact that the poverty of the soil keeps him a poor man is a little softened by circumstances which make it easier for him to be a proud man. This feeling is deep-rooted and genuine, and not to be confused with sentimentality. Any plan for rehabilitation of the Highlands which ignores it would work against the grain.

However, no man can live by pride alone, and his lands yield the Gael little else. Unless progress is to place the deadening stamp of uniformity on all the peoples of the earth, the spiritual and cultural identities of each must be developed, and it is as unfortunate for the pure Celtic strain to recede in Scotland as it would be in Ireland or Wales. While the clan retained its own lands there was enough, if not abundance, of the staple things for every man. When it lost them—how it did so is a matter to be explained later—the Gael was left to get out or to die. Even where a bare existence remained possible, to those few whom the lands under the new system of ownership could maintain as ghillies or servants, a weekly wage took the place of the ancient tribal economic system. The outcome was the usual one in cases of interference by the commercial system in primitive ones—the equilibrium was thrown out, and health and morale deteriorated. Canned meats, imported city bread, cheap clothing have penetrated to every croft, ousting the mutton and oats and wool which once nourished one of the most virile races on earth. This is a social problem which will be dealt with in another place, but it must be stressed here that the vitality and fertility of the Gael have been lowered far below danger-mark, and that this has set in motion a vicious circle which has impaired initiative and is altering the characteristics of the race.

The other basic loyalty of the Gael is the clan. By nature, the clan is a family rather than a tribe, a family sprung from a common ancestor, real or traditional, living in a patriarchal system, in which the chief takes the part of a kind of elder brother. It is important for an understanding of the Gael to realize that the chief is not a ruler of a higher caste. He is not the representative of the 'upper classes' of the Highlands, but the representative of the group of clansmen who bear his name. Fundamentally the society of the Highlands is a classless society, in which the division is not between rich and poor, but between name and name; and if southerners have sometimes shown scorn for a system of barbarous tribalism happily scotched by law and order and the central government in 1746, the Highlander may perhaps be forgiven if he wonders occasionally why horizontal social divisions should be deemed more civilized than vertical. It must be emphasized, too, that this relationship of clan and chief persists. The dispersal of the clansmen to the ends of the earth may have weakened, but has not broken it. There is still for a chief the deference due to the head of a family, or to a leader, but no subservience, and much of the good manners which southerners wonder at in the 'peasants' of the north springs from this relationship. There is mutual respect. There is mutual pride: the clan's in the chief who embodies the family, its traditions, and its lands, the chief's in the well-being, health, and prosperity of his 'children'. Indeed, there is an actual blood relationship between them, though the link may lie far back. And through the chief there is blood relationship to the Ard Righ Albann— the King himself—which explains an ancient Scots boast, quoted by Erasmus. The behaviour of some chiefs towards their clans at the time of the evictions might be thought to have shaken the system to its foundations; but it is precisely because the bond is one of kinship that in most parts of the Highlands the men still look for leadership to their chief. On the one hand, there is an equality of status and a fellowship that are in the best traditions of democracy; but on the other, there is an absence of the sense of citizenship deep-rooted among the peoples who for long came under the sway of Rome.

In spite of a glint of broadswords and a shrill of pibrochs out of the past, there is in the Gael a core of gentleness which too often is mere softness. It is in the very cadences of his speech. It warms his traditional courtesy and hospitality with charm; but on the other hand, because of it, too often that courtesy means nothing more than a following of the line of least resistance. It inspires a heritage of lovely literature and song, but it prevents the Gael from pursuing and developing his heritage as the Welshman or the Irishman has done. He will thrust it aside in a blaze of enthusiasm for some lost cause, and then tamely subside when the enthusiasm has died and adversity stares him in the face. It is the leaven which his brother Lowlander sorely needs; but in the end it has betrayed the Gael and opened the way for southern dominance, whether by sword or by lawyer's writ.

If the Gael has a soft core, the Lowlander has a core like flint.

There are many sorts of Lowlander, but the one quality common to them all is their durability. It has been the guarantee of their survival through six and a half centuries and has become their dominant feature as armour-plate is the dominant feature of a battleship. All their qualities, good and bad, derive from it, for the centuries have left them little else. English aggression, Calvinism, and the Industrial Revolution are generally represented as the three factors which have made them hard, but this seems to be a needless complication: the Scottish brand of Calvinism was an effect of character and not a cause, and to an extent the grim results of industrialism also flowed from the uncompromising spirit and ruthless combativeness without which the attentions of the Plantagenets and their successors would have destroyed the Scots. The first Edward's title, *Malleus Scotorum*, is doubly fitting, for he was the hammer which began the toughening process.

The hard core of the Lowlander contains, pent up within,

II. SCOTTISH TYPES

1. HIGHLAND CROFTER
   (*Alan Reiach*)

2. LOWLAND MINER
   (*Alan Reiach*)

3. HEBRIDEAN WOMAN
   (*Robert M. Adam*)

4. EAST COAST FISHERMAN
   (*From 'North Sea' by G.P.O. Film Unit*)

an inner core of smouldering, dark violence which has been the dominating force in Scottish history and which underlies most of the outstanding achievements of the Scottish people. From it derived the power to return the Plantagenets and the Tudors blow for blow, although England was rich and strong and Scotland without resources. It enabled the Bruce to collect from a devastated and occupied country the means to throw out the invader and within a few years to force Christendom to recognize him as the king of a free people. It produced the Covenanters, their ruthlessness and their courage, as it produced the determination of the remarkable stand for Church against State made by the seceding ministers in the famous General Assembly of 1843. It was the motive power of the grimly successful exploitation of Scotland's mineral wealth on which the Industrial Revolution had its foundation, and it is the chief quality through which Scots have in disproportionate numbers 'made their way in the world', to the envy and sometimes just indignation of their rivals. It may be that at the heart of this is a trace of the Celtic fire, transmuted by the metal encasing it—the metal of Saxon, of Briton, of Norman, of Fleming—into an element infinitely more fierce and more enduring. Its presence imbued the Lowlander with the energy that made him the really dangerous fighting man, ferocious in his dourness, implacable as he was slow to rouse. There is no white flame to it, bright but easily quenched, like the flame of the Celtic fire, but a deceptive, lava-like remorselessness and intensity, not only unspectacular but in some guises hideous, as when it seared the way to prosperity a hundred years ago under a scum of slums and exploitation. That this age-old violence should have in any way derived from a book compiled in the sixteenth century by a young man far away in Geneva is difficult to believe.

Freedom has been the one consistent loyalty of the Lowlander. Like the Russians, the Czechs, the Poles, or the Norwegians to-day, he has been willing to pay for the hope of it with everything he had. His pursuit of it has sometimes so narrowed his vision that in gaining one freedom he has lost another, as when the intensity of his hatred of Rome drove him into the bigotry of the opposite extreme, so that, paradoxically, his aggressive independence must be bracketed with narrowness of outlook. The commonest instance of this has been recurrent ever since he found he had riches under his feet. He had been a poor man robbed of what little he possessed over a period of so many generations that, when he found in his coal and iron the means to free himself from his traditional condition of poor relation among his neighbour peoples, only one goal seemed to him worth while—wealth. Wealth seemed to spell freedom from all sorts of petty humiliations. This mistaken idea of the value of property was not, of course, in the nineteenth century confined to Scotsmen; but the Scot pursued it with his characteristic singleness of purpose. It was the one achievement of that generation, a dismal monument to erect out of new-won power in a country in which there was little man-made loveliness. Again, a new thraldom had been entered into. . . . And so the grim thrusting toward freedom went on, this way and that, regardless of real happiness, while other more leisurely nations found their happiness by the way.

The Lowlander's individualism is an aspect of the pursuit of freedom by his people as a whole. As the Highlander will always agree with you, whatever he may really be thinking, so the Lowlander will usually disagree, to assert his independence. He is jealous of his rights, and he is also notoriously argumentative. This last trait has been attributed to centuries of theological wrangling. Again the cart has been put before the horse, for the weight of evidence would seem to suggest that the stubborn, wordy aggressiveness of the Lowlander down to the present day is a legacy of the long fight with more lethal weapons against endless encroachment on his rights—material, political, and spiritual. Also, it is another outlet for the smouldering violence in his nature already mentioned.

His individualism has powerfully shaped his political tendencies, for where the clan system and tradition drew the Highlands towards conservatism, Border history stamped the Lowlander with a brand of liberalism which the most revolutionary trends of political thought basically have done little to change. Aggressive vociferousness has caused timid people abroad to brand the Clyde as 'red' in the sense of communist; but the Clyde is probably the last place in Europe that would yield up its dour individualism. As remarked elsewhere, the Clyde when called upon 'went to it' in a manner astonishing in a rusty machine long lying derelict on the scrap-heap. But,

there is a grim side to the individualism and liberalism of the
Lowlander, for they were the root and inspiration of the cut-
throat economics which had their triumph under the banner
of freedom about a century ago. At a critical phase, Adam
Smith's *Wealth of Nations* sanctioned the long struggle of the
Lowlander for equal opportunity. Just as two centuries earlier
Calvin's *Institutes* had been borne aloft as sanction for fanati-
cism in the grasp of the Lowland Scot, who exalted dogma above
ethics, so the bible of free trade was used to exalt a bare theory
of economics above ethics. This resulted in the starkest pluto-
cracy ever known. Not only did it drag into slavery and
degradation much of the remnant of the Gaelic people in the
nineteenth century, but it ended for many generations the
Lowlander's own long-deferred hope of regeneration and the
advancement of his culture.

This crude side of the Lowlander—more especially the
industrial Lowlander, or about half the total population of
Scotland—has in places become veneered with an imported
culture, so that a southerner might live in the great cities and
not find them greatly more crude than the industrial cities of
England. But the crudity is there, even in the fabric of the
buildings. The ultimate effect of an English city, under its
coat of grime, may be as drab or more drab. Its attempts to
preserve amenity may be pathetic and ludicrous and misguided;
but the vast industrial areas of Scottish cities and towns make
no attempt at all and remain solidly and indestructibly dismal.
Even in the Black Country of England there are glimpses of
cheerful effort with paint-pot and window-box, where the
same sort of town between Forth and Clyde remains stubbornly grim. In the villages, the contrast is of course even more
marked. Almost always placed in lovelier surroundings than
its English counterpart, the Scottish village too often glowers
back at them gracelessly and distrustfully, except where
obvious function has made it forget itself, as in the Fife coast
fishing-ports or in exceptional localities such as the prosperous
parishes between Tinto and the Pentland Hills. Throughout most of the Lowlands and notably in the towns, there is
the same gracelessness in the manners of the people. There is
none of the ease and mellowness of a race that is sure of itself.
There are great depths of good-heartedness, but they seldom
well to the surface in a show of consideration or simple polite-

ness. Speech is unlovely. In the towns, the fine, expressive old dialect of 'braid Scots' has been forgotten and replaced by slovenly and debased varieties of English. Even in the country it has been vulgarized and vitiated by the refusal of the well-to-do and professional people to use it, with the result it is thought 'ungenteel' and falls back into association with oaths and expletives. Social habits have similarly fallen away. I am unable to follow the argument by which some writers pin the blame for the Scottish public house upon the licensing laws. The Lowlander's crudity in his drinking habits has the same dark background as all his other shortcomings in the sphere of the arts of living. When he drinks, he does not, like the Frenchman, savour at leisure the fruits of his own good earth and labour, nor does he do it to find forgetfulness: he drinks and gets unpleasantly drunk simply because the Lowlands have never had the chance to relax and discover the true meaning of leisure. In his cups, he becomes sentimental. It is a measure of the genius of Burns that he had all the vices and the sentiments of the Lowlander to excess and made great poetry out of them without ever falling into the perils of the maudlin sentimentality he must have known so well. The stature of his genius saved him, as the stature of Scott's saved him, from the worst perils of romanticism. And just as the legacy of Scott proved a Pandora's Box to the eager romantics who followed him, so the legacy of Burns has proved to the Lowland sentimentalists throughout the generations since his time. Burns' Night is kept as the chief festival of the Lowland Scot in every part of the world. Intended to commemorate a great name, frequently it succeeds only in perpetuating an uncouthness of feeling which Burns so delicately and so splendidly avoided.

There are two aspects of Lowland character which are notoriously misrepresented outside Scotland: the traditional 'meanness' and 'lack of humour'. The Lowlander is cautious. His country has always been a poor country by English or Continental standards. Where other soils provided not only more than enough to eat, but an abundance of fruits and wine which caused superabundance and even waste to become tokens of hospitality, the Lowlander had often barely enough to nourish his family and himself, so that waste became a cardinal sin. Industrial prosperity did not last long enough to alter this, although the industrial west is noticeably more lavish than the east. But right down to this day, Scotland has never possessed the surplus wealth which enables a man to enjoy throwing money or property away as a gesture. On the other hand, his native caution sees to it that the stranger also gets value for what he spends on him, and his invitation is never a careless and meaningless thing. And there is nothing casual in his welcome: it is pondered and sincere and warm, especially where it is thought to be needed, as thousands of Poles and Norwegians and Americans have testified in the past four years. . . . The misconception about his humour is less easily righted, because humour is essentially a national thing. Sydney Smith is generally blamed for discrediting Scots humour with his remark about the surgical operation, but the sardonic subtleties of the Lowland Scots joke could never appeal to the English sense of fun. It is one of the Englishman's most superb assets that he can discover a bright side to the most adverse circumstance—he by-passes adversity and takes it in the rear, so to say, and refuses to be cowed by its grisly frontal aspect. He would turn the Devil, if he met him, into a comic figure of the music-hall stage. The Scot, on the contrary, would find the Devil of absorbing interest *qua* devil. Instead of turning him into a figure of fun, he would accept him as a being of equal status and attempt to outdo him with a series of richly witty and profoundly gruesome stories of death and damnation. The average Englishman, I think, likes his joke to be obvious enough to produce the maximum amount of hilarity from the company; whereas the Scot tends to measure the success of his joke by the length of time others take to see it—always supposing the point to be a good one—and prefers his reward in profound chuckles rather than in loud laughter.

If the Lowlander's generosity and humour have been under-estimated, his feeling for religion and for learning have been misrepresented in quite a different way. The strictness of the Knoxian Sabbath is misleading: it has little in common with the fervour of religious belief in other parts of the world, but springs from a deep intellectual conviction of the need to discipline the flesh. Unlike the Gael, the Lowlander has a distrust of blind devotion. Zeal for a cause, yes—but he must be convinced of the cause. For other peoples religious belief may be something unquestionable and beyond the reach of argument; but to the typical Lowland Scot nothing—least of all religion—is beyond argument, and the Deity is by no means an unmentionable and unapproachable power communion with whom demands the intervention of a priest, but an authority to whom each individual can and must himself take his pleas. This, of course, is of the essence of Calvinism. Not Calvinism, however, but the far older spirit of independence is at the root of the Lowlander's attitude. His kings fought the attempts of England to impose her ecclesiastics between the Scottish Church and Rome; and, that issue settled, the people fought both Rome and England for their right to commune direct with God. An assessment of the struggle is left for another page. It remains one of the basic moulding factors of the Lowland character. No matter what the decline in the number of church worshippers, no matter how the strict forms of worship are modified, the Kirk of the Covenant is still present in the conscience of the Lowlander.

As to the feeling for learning, the outside world's impression has been coloured by the appealing picture of the 'lad o' pairts' with his bag of oatmeal, making good at the college in the distant city. The picture is soundly based on fact. In essentials, it can still be seen in the university cities, omitting the bag of oatmeal. It has been and remains a great Scottish tradition of equal opportunity for all—a tradition which is supported by the warm co-operation of parents, teachers, and the authorities who administer the system of education. The result of it is that a greater proportion of Scots, probably, than of any other people can boast of a higher education in the purely academic sense. This is at least as true of the Highlands as of the Lowlands. The false feature of the picture is in the underlying motive. Too seldom is this an ambition to enjoy a deeper culture, too often is it a sheer desire for betterment, financial and social. Earlier than others, the Scots saw opportunities of independence in the professions, and for more than a century now it has been the dream of parents who were themselves denied the best chances to see their son a minister of the Church, or failing that, a doctor or a schoolmaster. The professions themselves benefited hugely by an influx of solid, healthy, vigorous material; but in the steady flush of their success, too many Scots were blinded to the real meaning of a liberal education.

Even sport to the Lowlander is a dour and serious business, which accounts for his rather phenomenal successes in the games of his choice. Indeed, his sports throw interesting light on many aspects of his character. His individualism is here quite overweighted by his determination to win and he produces a degree of co-operation which he rarely shows in other fields. Faultless team-work is counted as the highest virtue, and the star performer with his 'fireworks' often produces no more than a glum stare and a shaking of heads among the spectators. An amusing instance of this was the dubiety with which the brilliant 'Oxford line' of three-quarters in the 'twenties was regarded by many an old Rugby veteran who clung to the tradition that victory for Scotland could ultimately lie only in solid 'spade-work' by the forwards. The national game is Association football. It continues throughout most of the year: cricket is a preserve mainly of the well-to-do. Football has been raised to a high level of scientific performance, and supporters are even more than in England fanatically absorbed in the form of their team, for the Scot at his weekends is less of a family man than the Englishman. In England, feeling rises to the pitch of its intensity over the Cup Final at Wembley, but in Scotland it is never so acute as between the spectators when the Rangers and the Celtic meet. This is more than a football match. It is a collision, symbolically, between the native Scot and the immense Irish influx to the Clyde basin, a collision between all they stand for. Feeling runs high, and there is more than just sporting give-and-take between the rival groups of spectators. The international match against the 'auld enemy', England, means much—far more than it does to an Englishman—but it is an academic affair, the rivalry blurred by the mists of history, compared with the outburst of pent-up feeling at a Rangers-Celtic match. Needless to say, first-class football is wholly professionalized—there is only one amateur team in the First Division of the Scottish League—and in the cities much of the working man's leisure is beguiled by the dismal attractions of the football pool and other forms of betting on the results of League games. Football has not the same hold upon the Highlands, but has largely replaced the native game of shinty, a very violent form of hockey. Rugby football greatly increased in popularity during the two wars. Formerly confined to pupils and former pupils of the Scots equivalent of public and grammar schools and, for some odd reason, to the Border towns, where the Association game and professionalism have never made headway, it has recently been adopted by a number of schools run by the education authorities. It has a more marked social status connotation than in England: Association football is played at none of the fee-paying schools. This is linked no doubt with the jealous regard for amateurism of the Scottish Rugby Union, which held its ground dourly against the introduction to the game of such professional or popularizing features as the numbering of players long after they had been conceded by the unions of other countries. It is significant that Hampden Park, the stronghold of the Association game, is in Glasgow, and Murrayfield, the Rugby stronghold, in Edinburgh.

The game with which Scotland's name is most closely linked is golf, and it is still a sport of the people north of the Border where in other countries it is a sport of the rich. It has been to Scotland what cricket has been to England—an art and a craft and a tradition which reflected the national character and in which all men sank their differences. The natural course was the great stretch of seaside turf, liberally served with hazards of sand-pit and bents, of the Fife, Lothian, Angus, and Ayrshire coasts, and the implements of the game were lovingly wrought by men who lived by those links and knew every lie to be found there. The 'professional' was a man who had served his apprenticeship to the game as a caddie; he divided his time between coaching beginners and making in his workshop the clubs that bore his name. The spread of the game throughout the world has altered much that was best in it—clubs are no longer tools with an individual character, courses no longer the grim, hazardous gauntlets which they were. I recommend A. G. Macdonell's witty pages on the subject in *My Scotland*. But not all the commercialization and notoriety has spoiled St. Andrews and the other Lowland centres as founts of golfing wisdom, because the secret of the game, as Macdonell says, is contained in two or three simple principles which the Lowland Scot hears drummed into him from the cradle, and the dazzling successes of the Americans have been built up and maintained only by the flow of dour and patient coaches from the haar-swept links of the Lowlands.

There is not in the Lowlands the comparative uniformity

of characteristics which the clan system maintained in the Highlands. A good deal is to be said for the contention that the people divide most naturally into occupational groups. For example, there is a distinctive Border group, based on sheep-farming and the woollen industry, productive of a fine yeoman type centred upon small towns in the river valleys, each town notable for a vigorous local patriotism. They are a shrewd, strong-minded, combative race, the Borderers, dour, but in a less grim sense than the men of the industrial belt and the east coast. The basin of the Clyde is the melting pot of Scotland. Here the native Lowlander and the Gael from the north meet with the Celt from Ireland, drawn by the magnet of heavy industry, and Lowland determination to succeed is fused with the quick wit of the Celt. In the Clyde valley the Scot is to be found most keenly alive to his opportunities, most vital, most aggressive, least sensitive to the vulgarities piled up by the industrial revolution. Here, too, he is most gregarious by nature. Between Clyde and Forth is another industrial community; but, tied to mining and with no direct intercourse with the outside world, it has not the resilience and vitality of the Clyde, has no clearly-defined identity and has a life with little colour and shape. The Lothians are largely an area of intelligent, prosperous farmers, with a sprinkling of mining communities. This was the one stronghold of the Angles in Scotland, and the Anglian penetration has been reinforced powerfully in recent years, for the number of Englishmen in business and official posts in Edinburgh is probably proportionately far greater than the number of Scots notoriously holding similar posts in London. Glasgow and a great area of the country round it are one within the common bond of their industries. Edinburgh is withdrawn and aloof, as capital cities are, but since she is divested of the functions of a capital her aloofness is inclined to seem foolish. She remains, however—despite the jibes of the vital, boisterous west—the only city equipped by temperament to do the honours of a capital. She has a certain lingering sense and tradition of service, as against the irrepressible commercial instinct. . . . North of the Forth is the well-marked community of Fife, hard-headed and prosperous, but 'thrawn' and high-tempered. With farmers in the east and miners in the west, there is a fringe of fishing villages not unlike the

Cornish fishing ports. North of the Tay again as far as the Mearns is another region of big farms, peopled by an uncompromising race which has had to contend with heavy soil and a merciless east wind. The only industrial centre, Dundee, is of the same grim temper—deriving wealth mainly from its connexion with the east through the curiously arid jute trade. North again is more prosperous farming in Aberdeenshire, where there is a considerable Norse admixture. Aberdeen itself is another aloof city at first sight but, even more than Edinburgh, a hospitable one at better acquaintance, though loyal to the north and not much impressed with what goes on to the south. Hard-bitten in the coastal area, this northern race grows—like the climate—milder and more expansive Moray-wards, until imperceptibly one comes again into the territory of the Gael beyond Nairn and up the valleys of the Findhorn and the Spey.

The Lowlander is almost as inveterate a seeker of his fortune abroad as the Gael, but the urge is different. The Gael, with his fine manners, his wit and his love of colour, is a natural cosmopolitan once the edges are rubbed off him; but I believe one of the Lowlander's chief motives in gravitating southwards is that never until he leaves his own people behind can he free himself of an incubus of self-consciousness and be at liberty to expand. In Lowland families, children as a rule have not been encouraged to speak their minds in the presence of their elders. It may be significant that in Scotland boys are often kept in short trousers to a much later age than is the case in England. Even in later life, when they have established themselves in their own villages and towns they feel the glances of appraisal following them and hear the whispers of 'Mphm—that'll be Sandy Thomson's Jimmie'. Only on foreign soil is independence to be found. Effects of this are both good and bad. There is probably a minimum of quick, rank growth and youthful foolishness; but transplanting sometimes induces a type of 'impossible Scot' not found at home. And it may be this diffidence in speech and to some extent even in initiative in family circles has had its effect on Scottish public life.

CHAPTER III

BACKGROUND: THE COUNTRY

THE inevitability of the greater part of Scotland's story can be seen in a glance at a good physical map.

Scotland—as Geikie long ago made clear—had begun her fight against unceasing and peculiarly ferocious invasion long before man made his appearance. She is the target of conflicting forces from west and east. From the west comes the fiercer onset by wind and rain and wave, but the defence in that quarter is stubborn, composed of immensely hard rock masses—crystalline schists and granites and basalts. In the east, the rather less powerful tides of the North Sea have an ally of great disintegrative power in the wider range of temperatures, and before this joint assault the opposition of soft sandstones, clays and shales is constantly defeated. The tattered appearance of the western coastline is misleading. Those long inroads of the sea are not inroads at all, but the sunken ends of the long glens formed by ruptures of the rock mass, and the numerous islands are not fragments of the land, but the summits of sunken mountains. The resistance to weathering of this rock mass of the Highlands can be gauged by the thinness of the soil. Over most of the area, except on the floors of the glens, the rock protrudes everywhere in knobs and scarps, and much of the covering even of the low-lying ground between the hills is not of soil but of peat formed by rotting aquatic plants which choked the lochs and tarns which once existed there. On the other hand, the sandstones and clays of the east have weathered and been converted to rich, loamy soils. This country is undulating, but hills are few and those smooth and rounded, except where an upthrust of igneous rock breaks through the sandstone, as at Stirling and Edinburgh. Off the east coast are few islands, but the softness of the land is marked here and there by rock stacks towering high and precarious from the sea, and by deep blow-holes and caves gouged far into the cliffs. The sea is constantly encroaching on the land. Or the destruction is even more rapid by wind-action on light, shifting sand, as at Barrie and Culbin. This slow, ceaseless war on two fronts is a low but significant undertone to the sharper conflicts which make up the main theme of Scotland's history.

Geological stress and strain have been broadly in the same direction as human thrust and counter-thrust—that is, south-east to north-west—which set up formations of folds and dislocations trending from south-west to north-east. The boldest of those features are the Great Glen, the Clyde-Kincardine line and the borders of the huge belt of Lower Silurian rocks forming the Southern Uplands. The soft fertile sandstone country of the east follows this diagnonal south-west-north-east trend and joins up with the carboniferous region in the narrow waist of the country to form a great, rich depression cut off to north and south by unfriendly regions difficult to pass. Open to the east, this rich depression was the natural goal of predatory migrations, tempting the German tribes as Northumbria and East Anglia tempted them. But, once settled, the invaders were almost cut off from their fellows settled in the east of England.

Meanwhile, the retreating Celt had made Scotland one of his last refuges. Its rugged, diagonal dislocations and folds had given him an ideal 'defence-in-depth' which he exploited adroitly against the Romans and all following invaders. Once within the system of hard, schistose strata with granitic outcrops that form the bulk of the Highlands, he possessed a network of fortifications which no weapons of the early days could reduce. The innumerable strong points could be held by a minimum of men. Individual valour could be exploited to the full against military organization and discipline. Communications—especially lateral communications—were superb. And it should be remembered that the Highlands, or a considerable part of them, were then clothed by the vast Caledonian Forest, not only in itself a barrier but an inducer of moisture which must have made the mountains even more a region of rain and mist and plunging torrents than they are to-day. Within this region the Celt lurked and learned from the Romans the lesson of unity and many lessons in tactics. To say that the Romans did not subdue the north because it was too barren to be worth their while is surely to fall a victim to the propaganda of the Roman tradition. They did not subdue it because the effort required would have been immense and the outcome indecisive. Later, against the Angles of Northumbria, whose realm extended deep into the rich central depression, the Celt had so far been given respite by the impregnability of his mountain fastness that he was able to take the initiative and carry his sway so far southward as to nip off the Anglian penetration. There were, of course, further waves of penetration, warlike and peaceful. But the disposition of mountainous barriers, the immense natural 'defence-in-depth' from the citadel of the Highlands to the outer barrier of the Southern Uplands, always enabled the race in possession to isolate and to some extent to absorb the incomers. Somehow those incomers, with whatever intent they may have arrived, had a tendency to face about and make common cause with the people among whom they had come. Both Wallace and Bruce were by ancestry Normans. Later, the innumerable Flemings who came to trade stayed to contribute some of the stoutest material to Scottish trading and craftsmanship. It is interesting to watch to-day the absorption of a considerable English population, especially in the Lothians —to note how within ten or twenty years an incoming Englishman's outlook becomes Scottish in a way that no Scot's would become English. It is a by-word that some of the most ardent Scots nationalists are Englishmen. No doubt many factors contribute to this; but not the least of the factors is the peculiar geographical isolation of Scotland, and particularly the entrenchment and compression of the most prosperous and populous part of the country between the defences of Highlands and Southern Uplands.

That durable formation of schists and granite and gneiss in the north-west also held off and limited a Norse influence which must otherwise have been great. The Orkney and Shetland Islands came wholly under the rule of the jarls, and the inhabitants of both groups to-day, while loyal Britons, will hardly acknowledge themselves as Scots. Racially, they are almost pure Norse. Norse rule extended equally to the Hebrides and Western seaboard, but the dependence of the Norsemen on their dominance of the sea while the Celt retained the advantage in the rugged hinterland prevented more than fleeting penetrations. The Norse influence on Celtic Scotland, apart from its large residue of place-names, was mainly one of stimulus to the Celtic stock.

The outstanding fact which emerges is that the central

III. CLIMATE

depression, the fertile lowland belt, is the cradle—or should it be called the melting-pot?—of the Scottish people as such. There, nourished on the sandstone and clay soils, and to some extent on the well-stocked waters of Forth and Tay successive waves of Teutonic peoples mingled with the fringes and remnants of the Celts and became fused with them. In the northern lowlands, in Strathmore and the Mearns, the Celt predominated, as the preponderance of Celtic place-names along the north-east coast commemorates, but environment and occupation did not encourage the Celtic features and institutions, and the north-easterner came to be as much a Lowlander in his way as the man of Lothian. The lowland belt is funnel shaped. The effect of a funnel is to compress whatever is poured into it by the sheer weight of what is superimposed, so that the physical attractions and restrictions of this region began and maintained by the Scottish people from within the country the consolidation and race conscious-ness to which Edward I and other English kings contributed from without.

Scotland is a country of much wider climatic differences than England. Prevailing warm south-westerly winds from the Atlantic, heavy with moisture, bring a high rainfall to the mountainous districts of the west. The east is colder and much drier, but the common occurrence of the chill sea-mists known locally as 'haars', during the spring especially, does much to offset the comparative freedom from rain. Morayshire and its coast is probably the region most free from wet weather and inclement winds, and indeed it has a climate perhaps as favoured as any in the British Isles. But the most notable feature of the Scottish climate is that its principal gradations are not from south to north, but from east to west. The mean annual temperature of the island of Islay is the same as that of the Isle of Wight, and the mildness of the winters along almost the entire western seaboard makes it possible in shel-tered places for palms, tree-ferns and even the Australian blue-gum tree not only to survive but to grow with some luxuriance. Yet only fifty miles to the east the telegraph wires may be sagging under the snows of a south-easterly blizzard. This vertical division of climates running counter to the diagonal racial division has also helped to blur the line of fusion between Highlander and Lowlander. It has had a bracing effect on the Celt of the north-east, inclining him to agriculture and industry from quite early times. No doubt it played a part in his rapid fusion with the incoming Lowland elements, with which he readily sided during the wars of independence. And in the western Lowlands, notably in Ayrshire, balmy airs and lush pasture and woodland have succeeded in softening a little the dour Lowlander. But the farther one goes from the line of fusion, either into Highlands or into Lowlands, the more are certain characteristics of Gael and Lowlander accentuated by geography and climate. In the far west and north, the native indolence of the Gael has been dangerously encouraged by the relaxing warmth and moisture, and the poverty of the soil has discouraged a race which is all too easily discouraged. In Wester Ross there are greener patches among the heather where past generations have attempted to sweeten the soil. Where the younger and more enterprising elements of the population have been drained away overseas, the remainder have made little attempt to maintain the ground won back to cultivation. Fierce winds and salt air have helped to turn the retreat into a rout. Conditions in the region would have tested all the dourness and energy of the Lowlander. Isolation, too—the very lateral defences which kept the Roman world and later waves of invasion at bay—has affected the natural ebullience of the Gael and cut him off from the moderate doses of foreign blood in his veins which he needs to invigorate him. At the other end of the country, the Lowlander has had transfusions from all kinds of 'donors'—Saxon, Angle, Norseman, Dane, and Fleming, to say nothing of more recent and constant infiltration— because his region had its doors open to east and south. His soil has repaid all the work he cared to put into it, and he had ready markets for his surpluses; yet the lateness of the seasons, the mists and grey skies which so often hung over his fields at harvest and the competition from a densening population always encouraged him to greater exertions and to new exercises of his ingenuity. Cold spurred his energies, but winters were rarely severe enough to hold up all operations for any length of time. But, where the Gael was genial, the chill east winds made the Lowlander grim-visaged, grudging in the expression of his inner warmth.

C

CHAPTER IV

BACKGROUND: THE BUILDING OF THE NATION

The Flow and the Ebb of Celtic Power

THE story of the Scottish nation may conveniently begin eleven hundred years ago, with that rare phenomenon, a counter-blow by the Celts against the forces which had pushed them westwards. In 844, Kenneth MacAlpin mounted the throne of the united kingdom of the Picts and Scots, ending a struggle which had lasted for three centuries, and the Celtic frontier began to creep southward again until in 1018 it ended at the Tweed.

Embryo Scotland was a colony of Scots from Ireland, who settled in Dalriada—now Argyllshire—about the year 500. The greater part of the country north of Forth belonged to the Picts, a fierce and somewhat mysterious race who, from their mountains, had defied even the Romans with success. For the rest, there were Britons extending from what is now Dumbarton as far as Cumberland; and from the Lothians southward were the Angles of Bernicia. The Scots early found a leader in a royal prince from Ireland, Columba. He was perhaps hardly the gentle and romantic figure of fable, winning over by his virtues the warrior Picts, but a determined missionary and a warrior himself, with the added advantage of being versed in the mental dexterities of Druid 'magic', if one reads Adamnan aright. Backed by his 'Christian soldiers', he confounded the priests of Brude, King of the Picts, much as Moses confounded the priests of Pharaoh at their tricks with rods and serpents. Brude was convinced, and converted. His people necessarily adopted the new faith of their king, if in practice they continued to follow the cult and superstitions of their ancient religion, while the themes of Christianity infiltrated among their old rites as they infiltrated among the designs of their art. But the high culture and civilization of Ireland began to influence the Picts, and the vanguard of returning Celtic power in the form of the missionaries of the Celtic Church at Iona brought a certain spiritual unity to the whole of the region which was to become Scotland. As soon as it had done its work of Christianization, the Celtic Church began to lose ground. At the Synod of Whitby in 664, Northumbria forsook Iona for Rome. Forty-six years later Naitan, King of the Picts, likewise gave his allegiance to the Roman form. In the words of Bede, 'Not long after, those monks also of the Scottish nation, who lived in the Island of Hii . . . were, by the assistance of Our Lord brought to the canonical observation of Easter, and the right mode of tonsure.' But neither Easter nor tonsure were the matters of real significance. The Celtic Church was a church of pious hermits, lacking in the unifying and cementing power of the Roman Church, and the kings of the Picts and of the Scots had learned the need for unity in the face of aggression from all sides. They had learned more quickly than the English, who were still a scarred and warring group of states. In 761 the Pict Angus MacFergus died virtually master of North Britain, and when Constantine I, King of the Picts, gave the Picts and the Scots a single ecclesiastical centre by transferring the monks of Iona to Dunkeld to ensure their safety from the descents of the Norsemen, no obstacle remained to the unification of Scottish and Pictish peoples under a ruler of their own blood.

Beset by enemies on all sides—Britons, Danes, and Angles—King Kenneth was fired by one ambition above all others: to drive southward into Lothian. He failed to annex it, and his successors for the next hundred years also failed—they had to face about and meet ferocious blows from the Norsemen under such formidable leaders as Olaf the White, Thorstein the Red, and Harald Harfagr, who seized the Orkneys and the Hebrides. Not until 1018 did the kingdom of the north, by this time known as Alba, succeed in turning defence into attack and defeated the Northumbrians at the Battle of Carham, on the Tweed, and so achieved King Kenneth's ambition, setting for all time the border of Scotland at the Tweed. This Alba was a purely Celtic kingdom. Its speech, perhaps with the exception of the Anglian Lothians, was Gaelic. The king ruled his provinces through seven *mormaers*, hereditary officers who in some cases had a dangerous degree of independence, and those under them the *toiseachs*, with military and later probably with sheriffs' powers. Even the Church had reverted largely to Celtic practices and had remained Celtic in much of its organization. In the northern part of the country the obscure sect of the Culdees, properly Keledei, maintained for centuries a hermit existence in the manner of the true faith of Iona.

I will return for a moment to that museum of Scots romanticism, Edinburgh Castle. Nothing moves the visitor more than the tale, told in the little Norman chapel, of how the sainted Queen Margaret heard the news of the death of her husband, Malcolm Canmore, and her eldest son, of how she herself died, of how her other sons bore her body out of the Castle under a 'haar', whilst her unnatural brother-in-law, Donald Bane, with his Highlanders beleaguered the Castle rock. All the softening influence of the Saxon queen on the rude Scots is recalled, precisely as it is recalled in the infant school history books. While the greatness of Queen Margaret is not to be denied, it is remarkable how fervid Scots to-day will take her side with eloquence, when the contemporary evidence shows that the Scots of the year 1093 hated everything she stood for, and that Donald Bane had the entire Celtic kingdom behind him when he came claiming the crown as his own with full justification by the Celtic law of tanistry.[1] That he came at the head of an army is not be wondered at. Margaret was a proud and resolute woman. She was a Saxon, regarded the Celt as a barbarian, had Saxonized the Celtic Church, spoke the Saxon tongue, had surrounded herself with Englishmen throughout her reign, had given her six sons Saxon names, and had gone far to remove the centre of gravity of Scotland from the Celtic north to the one Anglian province in Scotland—Lothian. That Margaret had brought many of the blessings of southern civilization with her from the Saxon Court to Scotland is undeniable, but it is only one side of the case—a people, like a man, may be excused if it resents blessings when it has to pay for them with cherished possessions. And the greatest of those possessions was leadership: never again were the Celts to be led by one of themselves. King Malcolm, the last of the pure Celtic line, save for Donald Bane and his brief rule, was beguiled by his queen into the acceptance of Anglo-Saxon ways, and the sons who ruled after him were sons of their mother.

The greatest of her sons was David I (1124–53), and his

[1] The Celtic system of succession, in which a collateral was preferred to a descendant.

SCOTLAND: AGRICULTURE AND FISHERIES
(with rainfall)

reign was outstanding in the Scottish story. Commerce grew
out of all recognition. The great trade with Flanders expanded,
and a vast influx of Flemings to the Lowland area followed.
Trade was stimulated by royal privileges granted to the
merchants, and the burghs for the first time began to take a
place of importance, encouraged by the bestowal of monopolies
and by the concession of certain rights such as that of choosing
their magistrates. There was comparative peace: Scotland
indeed became a sanctuary for refugees. Fine abbeys rose
throughout the length of the country—David is famed as 'a
sair sanct for the Crown'—and the dress and manners of the
people, in the Lowlands at least, conformed more to European
standards. The cost of all this was a new disunity—the growth
of a ruling class grouped under the King, alien to the people,
and especially to the great Celtic community. This ruling
class was Norman. The Normans never conquered Scotland;
they were given lands and power by the Scots kings, and in
return supported the kings through the efficient organization
of the feudal system which they brought with them. Some of
the greatest families in Scottish history had their beginning at
this time. Norman castles arose to maintain the power of the
new rulers, and with little struggle the people came to accept
them. Many Celtic chiefs conformed, siding with the new-
comers and conforming with their customs in order to maintain their personal power. Other Celts, notably Angus, the
Earl of Moray, resisted: it is significant that David looked
beyond the borders of his country for support and brought in
feudal barons from England to help him defend the feudal
machine in Scotland against the resentment of the Scots. But,
on the whole, increasing prosperity blinded the people to what
was happening to them. In the Lowlands, they even exchanged
their Gaelic speech for English, submitting to a subtle conquest
as the Highlands were to do six centuries later.

The Struggle for Independence

The obvious question arises: with the Scots' submission to
Norman domination, how is it that Scotland and England
did not fuse into one nation?

An explanation is to be found in the peculiarities of feudal
land-tenure. Scottish nobles did homage to the King of

Scotland for the lands they held north of the Border; but the King of Scots himself had extensive possessions south of the Border, and for those he owed allegiance to the King of England. From time to time, the English Kings tried to interpret the Scots King's homage in a wider sense, and by forged documents tried to prove the homage was due for the Kingdom of Scotland itself. In 1251 the boy king, Alexander III, did homage to Henry III for his English estates, and Henry tried to trick the boy into swearing the greater homage, but without success; and it is to Henry's credit that he took a benevolent attitude. A prosperous reign followed. Norse dominion over the Hebrides was shattered at the Battle of Largs in 1263, papal attempts to tighten control over the Scottish Church were also frustrated, and there was justice and wealth throughout the country. But in the autumn of 1275, on a black, wild night, Alexander fell to his death over the cliffs at Kinghorn, and his granddaughter, the infant Margaret of Norway, became Queen. She died on her way to Scotland.

Instantly Robert Bruce, Earl of Annandale, closely related to the late King, asked the protection of his feudal overlord in England, Edward I, and claimed the throne. Edward seized his opportunity. He claimed to be Lord Paramount of Scotland. Confronted by an army, the Anglo-Norman nobles of Scotland assented. The two chief candidates for the Scottish Crown, both Anglo-Norman nobles with some Celtic royal blood in their veins, were Bruce and John Balliol, and Edward—probably with justice—gave his award to Balliol, who meekly swore fealty to him and was crowned at Scone. Edward's subsequent behaviour was in a striking degree like the behaviour of Adolf Hitler towards his neighbour states. Starting from one monstrous false premise, his claim to over-lordship, he preserved a pedantic fiction of legality for a series of tyrannical measures against the Scots, until even the weak quisling Balliol demurred, was summoned to appear before his suzerain and miserably returned to Scotland with orders to carry out further humiliating demands upon the Scottish people. But the Scots were roused beyond endurance. A council at Scone voted the forfeiture of the Scottish estates of all Englishmen at Court and Balliol was forced to inagurate the celebrated Franco-Scottish alliance. A Scottish army invaded England. Edward in revenge put Berwick to the sword. The chief castles of the Lowlands fell to him, and Balliol in his presence abdicated. The Celtic Stone of Destiny Edward carried off from Scone to Westminster Abbey where it now rests under the Coronation Chair, and the Normanized Barons hastily denied their country's right to independence by putting their signatures to the Ragman Roll.

Betrayed by their alien rulers, the Scots found a hero to lead them. Sheer, selfless heroes are not numerous in history —Robert Bruce himself was as calculating as he was courageous. But William Wallace had no self-interested motive for leading the Scots people against the English, unless the fabled murder of his wife by the English be accepted as such motive. He was of the Norman ruling caste, if a humble member, and it would be interesting to know what caused him to throw in his lot with the commons of Scotland; but, once committed, he never turned aside. By excellent generalship, he drove the invaders from many of their strongholds. In the end, however, the longbowmen defeated him and, when he had died a traitor's death, his head was flaunted on London Bridge.

Wallace did not die in vain. His resistance put new hope and determination into the Scots, and they found another champion in Robert Bruce. Also a Norman baron, and a trusted supporter of Edward, he outlawed himself from his caste and at the same time from Rome by killing an enemy, the Red Comyn, in the church of the Minorite Friars at Dumfries in 1306. The Scottish Church even under Rome was as fiercely independent as the Scottish people: both instantly gave their support to Bruce, and he was crowned at Scone before the papal excommunication or the wrath of Edward could reach him. He spent a winter in hiding. Then, gathering his forces, he met the Earl of Pembroke and defeated him at Loudoun Hill. He moved on to meet the avenging army of Edward, when suddenly the old King died. A further period of gathering strength followed, and from 1308 to 1313 Bruce, with supporters such as his brother Edward and the famed Black Douglas, systematically rooted out his enemies— those of his countrymen who had been sympathizers of Comyn, and also the English garrisons of the great Scots castles. Edward II's actions were futile; but in 1314 he gathered an army of great strength, with engines of war and the great supply-trains needed to combat the traditional 'scorched-earth' policy of the Scots, even with a poet to sing of the triumph. The moment was critical. King Robert's successes had been due to his cunning as a guerrilla fighter; now he must engage in a pitched battle. But his cunning did not desert him. Inferior in numbers as one to two, he took up a position protected by bog and stream, broke up the English archery by a well-timed cavalry charge and let Edward's heavily-armed knights founder and die between the Scottish spearmen and a 'minefield' of pitfalls and calthrops. Edward barely escaped from Bannockburn with his life. For the remainder of Bruce's reign the initiative lay with the Scots, who time and again carried the offensive into England and even made an unsuccessful bid to secure Ireland. Papal frowns were exchanged for papal favours. Scotland knew a triumphant unity—attempts to see a division between Celtic Highlands and Saxon Lowlands at this stage have no foundation in fact—and Bruce in 1326 invited representatives of the burghs to attend the Great Council of his feudal tenants, a first step towards the representation of the commons in the Scottish Parliament. But his achievement above all others is that in the twenty-three years of his reign he built Scottish independence upon such firm foundations that not all the foolishness of his son, David II, weakened it. Edward III made incursions like his grandfather's and left smoking ruin behind him in the Lowlands; he set up for a period in Scotland another quisling of the Balliol line; he even held King David himself to ransom for eleven years. But none of these misfortunes—even with the horror of the Black Death added to them—in any way injured the buoyancy and confidence with which the Scots now faced the English. They had forgotten the military wisdom of the Bruce; but his spirit remained alive among them.

Scotland in Independence

Scotland's independence was assured, but she lay a poor and stricken nation, and the struggle against England gave place to the internal struggle between Crown and Barons which England and France also underwent. A new dynasty ruled: the Stewarts. In 1371, David II had died without heir, and his nephew Robert, the High Steward, succeeded him.

The first two Stewarts were weak men, no longer young when they came to the throne, and men of violence did much as they liked. The Douglases ranged as far as Ireland and made frequent forays into England, rousing Richard II to an expedition of revenge in which he burned Edinburgh, Perth, and Dundee and reduced to blackened shells some of the greatest of the Border abbeys, including Melrose. In the north, King Robert III's own brother, the Wolf of Badenoch, and his illegitimate sons terrorized Moray and Angus, while a feud between Clan Chattan and Clan Cameron was actually decided on the Inches of Perth at the King's suggestion in a bloody fight to the death by thirty picked warriors on either side. The King's eldest son died at Falkland—traditionally by the hand of the Duke of Albany, the regent-to-be—and to escape his fate the Prince James, his brother, was sent by sea to France, only to fall into the hands of Henry IV of England.

Romance clings to the name of Stewart, not unjustifiably. The tale of the prisoner in England, writing verses in his tower to Joan Beaufort in the garden under his window, was immortalized by the prisoner himself in *The Kingis Quair*, and when —ransomed by his countrymen—he returned to Scotland in 1424 as James I, with Joan Beaufort as his Queen, he carried with him the experience of eighteen years of observation, not only of the English, but of the culture and the mode of chivalry in France. His first task, as he said himself, was to 'make the key keep the castle and the bracken-bush the cow'. He crushed the unruly Lord of the Isles, receiving his submission in a dramatic scene at Holyrood. He beheaded his enemy, Albany. He was merciless in his measures to establish his position. But he also strove to establish something like the parliamentary system which he had seen in England, requiring the attendance of two 'wise men' from each shire to relieve the lesser barons, introduced a system of statute law and a permanent body of Lords of Session to administer the law. And he promulgated a wide range of social decrees affecting agriculture, commerce, the sick. No king so vigorous, and indeed so excellent, had sat on the Scottish throne for a hundred years. His fault lay in statecraft, for he recklessly made enemies—among the barons by the ruthlessness with which he put down their power, and among the commons by the taxation which he tried to enforce upon them. His baronial enemies took their revenge: they assassinated him in a cellar of the Blackfriars Monastery at Perth at Christmas, 1437.

The minority of James II brought to a head the rivalry and enmity of the most powerful of the baronial families, the house of Douglas. At the notorious Black Dinner in Edinburgh Castle, in the presence of the little King, the young Earl of Douglas and his brother were seized by the Keeper of the Castle and put to death. James, when he came to the throne, punished those responsible, but the new Earl continued to intrigue against him. The power of this Border family was immense, its prestige, popularity and magnificence greater than the King's. Either the Douglases or the Stewarts must fall. James tried to settle the question himself. He invited the Earl to dine with him at Stirling, argued with him, lost his temper and ran him through with his sword. Thereafter he invaded the country of his victim, got his Parliament to attaint the family and brought the House of Douglas down in ruin. This deed alone stands out in his reign, although he was a good ruler and continued the legislation of his father. In 1455, at the siege of Roxburgh Castle, the explosion of a cannon brought about his death.

Although the nobles were yet to overthrow a king, never again did one of them achieve the strength to challenge the House of Stewart. The new minority brought no disaster on the country, in spite of danger from the conflagration of the Wars of the Roses raging south of the Border. The guiding hand in the difficult years was that of the great Bishop Kennedy of St. Andrews, and his policy was to support the Lancastrians, whose leader, Henry VI, with his Queen, Margaret of Anjou, took refuge in Scotland after their defeat at Towton in 1461. However, when the Yorkist Edward IV came to terms with the King of France, Kennedy prolonged peace and prosperity by coming to terms with Edward also. James III, when he came to rule, proved to be a man unhappily born into the wrong age. His dislike for war and politics and for the fierce tension at which his father and grandfather had had to live should find a sympathetic response to-day, but most historians seem to share the contempt of his own times and relish the incident of the hanging of the King's friends from the bridge at Lauder by jealous barons. There is little evidence that the 'offence' was more than the intelligent companionship of commoners which the King had the oddity to prefer to the intrigues and crude ambitions of his barons, but no doubt Archibald Bell-the-Cat and his friends could see none but a sinister motive in the elevation of a plain architect to the Earldom of Mar. Inevitably, James forfeited his crown. In an attempt to crush the nobles arrayed against him at Sauchieburn, he found defeat and then death under the knife of an assassin. The great events of his reign were not his achievements. The transference of Orkney and Shetland from Norway to the Crown of Scotland in 1472 was due to a default in his marriage settlement after he had wed the daughter of King Christian I. In the same year, the Pope erected St. Andrews into an archiepiscopal see, thus ending for all time the ancient claim of the archbishopric of York to jurisdiction over the Scottish Church. But sumptuary laws show the time to have been one of rising prosperity.

James IV's reign is the brief zenith of the Stewart rule. For Scotland, it closed the door on the Middle Ages and with a fanfare of silver trumpets ushered in the Renaissance. The splendour of it all is generally focused on the King himself, and—if half the tales of him are true—not without justification. In the meadow by the Nor' loch under the crags of the Castle of Edinburgh the lists are set out, and the knights ride courses at one another for the honour of their ladies and a lance tipped with Scottish gold, while all about there is wit and laughter, silks of France and Flanders and the red wine brought by Scottish vessels from Bordeaux. James jests in Spanish with Pedro de Ayala, Ambassador of Ferdinand and Isabella, exchanges a word in Gaelic with some chieftain from the north. Margaret Tudor, his Queen, is there, and Will Dunbar, the court poet, pondering some sequel to *The Thistle and the Rose*, which saluted his master's wedding in jewelled verse. . . . Or the scene changes to a dark, vaulted room where the King, intent and eager, leans across the shoulder of his alchemist to watch the vapours coiling in his still, or to a foundry where, hands on hips and the glare of furnace reddening his face, he watches the casting of the cannon and dreams of triumphs over Henry VIII. . . . For the first time, a Scottish king owned a good fleet, with the *Great Michael*, the largest ship afloat, and in Sir Andrew Wood of Largo a sea-dog who had tried his teeth on the best seamen of Henry and come off best in the face of heavy odds. He had a prosperous kingdom, too. It had a fine trade across the North Sea and a clearing-house of its own for merchandise in the Low Countries—the Scots Staple at Campvere. And it was a secure kingdom within: the barons had been reduced to obedience and even the Lord of the Isles had given up his title to the King. As to learning, not only was there wealth of scholars and poets, but an education act required barons and freemen to send their sons to school, and a third university—Aberdeen—had been added to St. Andrews and Glasgow, while the Royal College of Surgeons of Edinburgh received its charter. There were excellent relations, too, with France and with Denmark. Indeed, with the possession of a marriage-tie with the old enemy, England, there seemed nothing to prevent this dawn of real prosperity and peace from ushering in a golden age; but the very chivalric virtues in the King which did so much to grace the kingdom were bound up with the daring and impatience and over-confidence which brought about his downfall. Throughout a large part of his reign James flirted foolishly with danger by harbouring the pretender Perkin Warbeck and granting him a handsome pension. So, in August, 1513, against sager advice but with the loyal support of all Scotland, for little more than a whim, he led the knighthood and spearmen of the country to defeat and extermination at Flodden.

The fifth James inherited the ability of the Stewarts, with a degree of honesty and steadfastness and goodwill towards his people that deserved better of fate. He had a great desire to improve the lot of the ordinary man and a curiosity which moved him to go among the people as one of themselves, but all the time he had to face the unscrupulous cunning of his uncle, Henry VIII. Henry had sacked the religious houses of England and cut himself off from Rome. He advised his nephew to do the same in Scotland, and the Scottish Church in its corruption deserved no better fate; but James revolted from such an act, and drew closer to his great cardinal, Beaton, as Henry deepened the gulf between himself and Wolsey. Henry retorted by trying to kidnap James and to revive the old fiction of suzerainty over Scotland. The Scottish barons betrayed their King, and in 1542 the army of James and Beaton met defeat at the Solway Moss. The King's sons had died. In the hour of defeat came the news of the birth of a daughter and James, turning his face to the wall, murmured his famous prophecy about the Scottish Crown: 'It cam wi' a lass and it will gang wi' a lass'. The lass was the infant Mary, to be Queen of Scots.

The War of Kirk and Crown

The alliance of the Crown and the Roman Catholic Church was intensified after the death of James: Mary of Guise, his Queen, became Queen-Regent, and she sent the little Queen to France, where she was married to the Dauphin, who became in name King Francis of Scotland. Reform was a powerful and popular movement, because of the corruption of the Church. Its leader, John Knox, had known the French galleys after capture at St. Andrews, where he had approved the murder of Cardinal Beaton by the Protestants in 1546 in revenge for the hanging and burning of George Wishart, and his hatred found outlet in an eloquence and persistence which made him a terrible enemy. England supported the Protestant Party, less because of her religious sympathies than because the King of France had advanced Mary's claim to the Crown of England.

In 1560, the death of Mary of Guise put the power utterly into the hands of the Protestants. With no Queen and no Regent in the country, the Protestant leaders, the Lords of the Congregation, summoned a Parliament, which accepted Knox's Confession of Faith forbidding the saying of Mass; and—contrary to the commonly distorted traditional tales of Knoxian ferocity—the death penalty was never exacted in the execution of this measure, and at a time, as Hume Brown pointed out, when religious persecution had drenched in blood Germany, France, Spain, and even England. But it meant in effect a dictatorship of the Kirk. It is true that the Protestant system of presbyteries, synods and a General Assembly meant in theory something like democratic representation in the conduct of affairs, but of course no man would have dared make heard his opinions in opposition to the decrees laid down through the ministers of the Kirk. However, there is no reason to think the people opposed the reformers. The struggle lay between the Kirk and the Crown, and Mary, who returned from France a widow in 1561, made a vigorous fight of it.

She fought, not with any view of overthrowing the Protestant religion, but to maintain herself amid a grisly network of plots and counter-plots, and above all against the machinations of Elizabeth, who in her turn had to maintain herself against the Roman Catholic world which would dearly have liked to see her throne occupied by her cousin and heir. Mary, indeed, had to depend largely on the Protestants. Even her husband, the vicious young scoundrel Darnley, schemed against her, for the murder of Mary's secretary, Rizzio, was a move towards securing the Crown of Scotland for himself. Another plot, which ended with the strangulation and blowing-up of Darnley himself at Kirk o' Field, at last brought about the downfall of the Queen. The Earl of Bothwell seems to have been the murderer, but he was acquitted and three months after the death of Darnley married Mary himself. Whatever the authenticity of the Casket Letters, there can be little doubt Mary was guilty of an infatuation, which dulled all her scruples, for the brutal, colourful Warden of the Borders who ended his days as a pirate. There is no doubt she was the victim of a plot involving some of the greatest names in Scotland. In a few weeks the Protestant Party had, at Lochleven, secured the throne for her son, and James VI was crowned at Stirling in the presence of John Knox. The King's—otherwise the Protestant—party ruled through a series of regents, among them two very strong men, the Earls of Moray and of Morton. They had to contend with a Queen's party of considerable strength. And when Mary escaped from Lochleven to become a captive in England, Elizabeth, secure in the possession of a powerful 'piece' with which to threaten the security of the Scottish King, no longer made any pretence of supporting the Protestants. Morton, moreover, was no real champion of the Kirk. He reintroduced a form of Episcopacy, in order to increase church revenues which, by a measure of 1561, were to be divided between clergy and Crown, and he opposed the power of the church courts. Knox was at the end of his fighting life; he died in 1572. A new champion of the Kirk arose in Andrew Melville, who became Principal in succession of the Universities of Glasgow and St. Andrews, and his great achievements were the Second Book of Discipline and the provision of the typical Presbyterian church courts. The Second Book of Discipline insisted that all ministers are equal, thus repudiating bishops, and that the temporal and spiritual jurisdictions are separate: both measures on which King James was shortly to join battle.

In 1578 James took over the power nominally. From the first he leaned towards Episcopacy, and the famous Ruthven Raid was an attempt to wrest him from the advisers who had determined that attitude—chief among them Esmé Stewart, Earl of Lennox. James never forgave the attempt, nor the boyish tears it had wrung from him. But the supreme factor which shaped his policy was the ambition to sit on the throne of England. England might return to the fold of Rome; yet, again, she might not. The precocious young King saw that the middle course of Episcopacy would commit him to neither extreme, but the influence which had to be resisted most stubbornly was Andrew Melville's, and he went the length of secretly sounding the Pope about the possibility of his becoming a Catholic. The Earl of Arran now acted as his chief adviser. However, Elizabeth, much alarmed at this turn of events, secured the Earl's downfall, and James decided that the wisest course in view of his ambition was to be her friend; and so faithful proved his friendship that when Elizabeth in 1587 executed her prisoner Mary, her son King James, now a step nearer still to the English throne, did no more than protest. And now, before he left Edinburgh for London, James tasted triumph over his arch-opponent, Andrew Melville, the man who had had the courage to call his sovereign 'God's sillie [simple] vassal' to his face. Threatening to remove Court, Privy Council and law courts from the capital if it opposed his will, James forced the Assembly to appoint bishops under the name of 'Commissioners' by persuading a committee to petition for the representation of ministers of the Kirk in Parliament. Only the Gowrie Conspiracy now lay between him and the achievement of his ambition: in 1600, according to James, the son of his old enemy, Ruthven, decoyed him alone into Gowrie House and would have killed him had not his attendants come to his aid and slain Ruthven and his brother first. The result avenged him well, and James's tale is perhaps best received as all Europe received it at the time —with raised eyebrows. In 1603, this wily, vain man, whose interests ranged from golf to demonology, left Scotland with crocodile tears in his eyes and mounted the throne of the Tudors.

As soon as he was King of England, James nursed the hope that he might reduce Scotland to the status of a northern county. Opposition among the nobles had been easily placated by the ceding of those Church lands which James V had scorned to cede, and the only power arrayed against him was the Kirk. Parliament in Scotland had never attained to anything resembling an organ through which the people might express their will, but James reduced its function to that of the Reichstag under Hitler and ruled Scotland—as he ruled England—through his Privy Council.

In Scotland, his will was executed, as he boasted, by a 'Clearke of the Counsell'. He attacked the Kirk by forbidding the General Assembly, and in doing this he did far more than if he had banned Parliament, for the Assembly was the effective Parliament. Unlike his son, he had the cunning not to attack the forms of service, and so he raised no hostility among the people. Andrew Melville was got rid of by a trick; James summoned him to London and treated him with all graciousness, himself taking some part in the theological arguments so dear to him, and then a frank remark of Melville's about what he considered popish forms in the English Church gave the King the opportunity to commit him to the Tower. The way lay open for the appointment of bishops. 'Perpetual Moderators' for each Presbytery had already been appointed at a meeting called by James, and with Melville out of the way, James announced that the meeting had been a General Assembly, and it was discovered that the 'Assembly' had arranged for synods and presbyteries to have perpetual moderators who should be members of the General Assembly. With typical adroitness, James bluffed the people at this point by pressing for stronger action against Roman Catholics. It only remained to call the bishops by their true style, and at a nominated Assembly in Glasgow in 1610 it was made an offence to preach the equality of the ministry—a measure which almost certainly had bribery behind it—and due consecration of the bishops by English bishops followed. But Presbytery survived. The Kirk Session remained the contact with the people. By this device and by his sparing of the form of service, popular wrath was kept at bay. Not until 1616 did James feel himself strong enough to interfere with the use of Knox's *Book of Common Order*; in 1617 he returned for the first time to Edinburgh and horrified it with his surplices, choristers and kneeling communicants; and in 1618 threw a challenge in the teeth of his countrymen in the shape of the Five Articles of Perth, which enforced certain Anglican forms. At last the Scottish people broke into revolt. Neither the most imperious threats nor the Court of High Commission could produce any effect on a nation-wide defiance. And with this situation unmoderated, the King died in 1625.

The War of Kirk and Crown—II

As Rait aptly remarks, James I made bishops possible in Scotland and Charles I made them impossible.

Charles had none of his father's guileful sense of just how far he could go with safety. He made episcopal government, under his own Royal Headship, the definite basis of the Church in Scotland, and had his will carried out even in such details as the wearing of the surplice. Archbishop Laud accompanied him to his coronation in Edinburgh in 1633, imperiously disregarding the Scottish traditions of worship; and the Lords Spiritual dominated the Parliament which followed, a Parliament which the King himself abruptly dissolved as soon as it passed the bills which he wanted, and before it could protest. Incredibly, Charles even alienated the nobles. This he did by the Act of Revocation, annulling all the royal grants of land since 1542—this with the worthy purpose of increasing the clergy's stipends, and the less worthy one of swelling his own coffers. This created an immense economic upheaval, and a deep and growing resentment among all, for the beneficiaries—the ministers—realized their benefits had been paid for by a new dependence on the King. But the match which brought about the explosion was the introduction of the new Prayer-Book, known as Laud's Liturgy, in 1637. The scene in St. Giles's Church in Edinburgh on 23rd July is world-famous—the tumult, the flying stools, the scream of 'Traitor, dost thou say Mass at my ear!' The reasons for it were that Knox's long-respected *Book of Common Order* had at last been ousted by a service-book suspected of Popery, introduced from England and imposed by a King who had usurped the place of 'Chryst Jesus the King, and his Kingdome the Kirk', in the words which Andrew Melville had used to James VI.

Now it was open war between the King and the Scots. Charles carried out the old royal threat and withdrew the Privy Council and the courts of law from Edinburgh. Petitions had been useless. The indignant people solemnly elected from among themselves a virtual Parliament, and met in the Parliament House, each of the Four Estates of the Realm sitting at a separate table, which gave the name of The Tables to the assembly. The Tables demanded the removal of bishops from the Council. Charles threatened to brand them with treason. The retort to this was the National Covenant, a document denouncing Popery, which forced the bishops to flee to England and the King to appoint a Commissioner in Scotland who proceeded to offer compromise followed by an attempt to divide the people by offering an alternative Covenant for their support. In November of this year, 1638, a General Assembly met in Glasgow. The King's Commissioner, weeping, dissolved it; but it continued to sit and set about a trial of the bishops which ended in their deposition and the excommunication of several. Not only was this war, but war with the sword. And the Scots were ready for it, with a great commander in Alexander Leslie, veteran hero of Gustavus Adolphus's wars. With tried troops like himself in his army, Leslie had the King at his mercy; but the last thing he wished to do was to humilitate his King, and the Pacification of Berwick brought about the disbanding of both armies. Charles tried to gain time to win English support; but English sympathies were with the Covenanters, and when war broke out again Leslie pressed south to Newcastle. Charles thought he must now be sure of English support and summoned the Long Parliament, only to find that the English looked on the Scots army of occupation as an assurance of their own liberties, and when Scottish Commissioners went to London it was to watch with keen pleasure the toppling down of the apparatus of despotic monarchy.

But the apparent common cause of the English and the Scots proved to be two causes, and incompatible ones. The deep grievance of the one people was the threat of the Divine Right to principles of civil government which had their roots in Magna Carta; of the other, the threat of the same to the Divine Right of Presbytery. The English abhorred absolutism of any kind; the Scots—or the dominant element among them

—wished to replace one absolutism by another. The furious momentum of the Lowlander has always tended to drive him to extremes. Scottish help was therefore offered at a price— establishment of Presbytery in England. Agreement was marked by the Solemn League and Covenant of 1643. Parliament, together with the Assembly of Divines, ratified it in England. The General Assembly ratified it for the Scots. The factor which persuaded the Commons was the Scottish army of 20,000 men, without which they were at the mercy of the King, but, as soon as Cromwell's New Model Army took the field and proved itself, the need for the Scots was gone and the vows of the Solemn League could be trampled under the boots of the Independents. And the 20,000 had to return north. James Graham, Marquis of Montrose, a brilliant general, had raised a Royalist force which included the men of the clans and, eluding danger after danger, had defeated the Covenanting forces sent against him until at length a son of the great Leslie caught and routed him at Philiphaugh with a butchery which for ever stained the standards of the Covenant. Then the King surrendered to the Scots. They tried to get him to sign the Covenant, but he would not. Three courses of action were possible: to take him back with them to Scotland, to let him escape, to surrender him to Cromwell. The first meant war with England over the person of a King who remained an enemy of Presbytery. The second meant trouble deferred. Only a lingering loyalty to the name of Stewart caused hesitation over the third, which was adopted with the condition that no harm should come to Charles. To say the Scots 'sold' their King is nonsense. The only money which passed was a portion of the arrears of pay which the Commons had guaranteed to the Scots for their help in England. Moreover, the English had never carried out the Solemn League. And when they broke their engagement by beheading Charles, pity and anger won all Scotland for the Stewarts. Their cause was taken up again by Montrose, but defeat and execution overtook him. The second Charles with facile pen signed both the National Covenant and the Solemn League and in 1650 landed in Scotland, but Cromwell ended his hopes by defeating Leslie at Dunbar. Division rent the country, for Charles's glib promises were mistrusted, but on New Year's Day of 1651 the Marquis of Argyll crowned him at

Scone. Cromwell came against him. Charles eluded him and marched with a Royalist army into England, but England shunned his cause and Cromwell put an end to his power at Worcester.

A form of union between England and Scotland followed, but there was no pretence of equality of status, and when the General Assembly attempted to meet in Edinburgh Cromwell's soldiery gave it as short shrift as the Protector himself gave to his Parliaments. The best that can be said of those few years is that there was peace in Scotland, with justice—no mean accomplishment; but for Burnet's claim of prosperity there seems to be little basis.

The 'covenanted' King Charles II soon showed his cynical indifference to the hopes of the Scots. 'Presbytery', he remarked, 'is not a religion for gentlemen.' He did not aim at his grandfather's policy of merely conjoining Presbytery and Episcopalianism, which had wisdom in it, as the Highlands and the north-east were Episcopalian: his object was the replacement of the one by the other. Lauderdale aided him, and James Sharp of Crail became Archbishop of St. Andrews. He struck at the very roots of the Kirk by making its lower courts dependent on the bishops, and through them upon his own will, and the ministers who stood out against this were driven from their parishes to the number of 271. From these sprang the 'Conventicles', open-air services of worship, and when the Government pursued them with military force the worshippers were driven to take up arms in defence of themselves. Persecution and torture turned extremists into fanatics, and the name of Whig or Whiggamore given to them is significant in its meaning of a driven beast. These Covenanters were a darkly violent sect—the history of the Lowlands made their emergence inevitable; but those who profess to find the sin on their side are best answered by calling attention to the words of their oppressor, Lauderdale: 'Would to God they would rebel, so that I might bring over an army of Irish Papists to cut all their throats.' And he brought them to revolt. In 1679, Archbishop Sharp was murdered on Magus Muir. A month later the Covenanters of the west defeated Graham of Claverhouse at Drumclog. Monmouth granted a generous indemnity after his victory over them at Bothwell Brig, but the Covenanters' reply was the fanatical Declaration of

Sanquhar, which disowned the King for his breaking of the Covenant. The Government pursued its unwisdom by taking a bloody revenge upon the sect of the 'Cameronians'. But when James VII and II succeeded his brother, his unconcealed leaning towards Rome drove the Episcopalians into the camp of all but the most fanatical Presbyterians, and the last victim of the persecutors of the Covenanters died in 1688. The fanatic sects were to hive off and become 'Cameronians', afterwards called Reformed Presbyterians, while the great moderate party of the Presbyterians in its negotiations with William and Mary achieved the long-coveted disestablishment of the Episcopalian Church in Scotland and the restoration of the Reformed Kirk in all but the Knoxian Confession, the place of which was taken by the Westminster Confession of Faith. Troubles were not ended, for Episcopalianism remained strong in the north, especially in the Highlands, where Stewart sympathies were keen, and here Jacobitism instantly arose and even won a transitory military victory at Killiecrankie. For a generation Whig ministers had short shrift in the more remote parishes of the north-west. But Presbytery represented the feelings of four Scots out of five, and incidents such as the Massacre of Glencoe and William's part in bringing about the disaster of the Darien Scheme soon stopped the danger of any real disunity north of the Tweed.

The Government Goes South

A Scottish Parliament possessed of real power emerges for the first time in 1690, for in that year William agreed to end the ancient council of the Lords of the Articles, which for three centuries had been the instrument of rule. William was the first semblance of a constitutional king, not only in England, but in Scotland. Anne had been agreed as his successor by both. But after Anne, failing an heir, who was to bind the two countries and their now-sovereign peoples? The Scots had age-long reason to fear to trust their spiritual independence to others, and their Parliament passed a Bill of Security to ensure itself a suitable succession and to impose on all Scots military training as a guarantee of their freedom. Anne's refusal of her assent to this threatening measure brought a murmur of republicanism from Scotland, led by the voice of

Fletcher of Saltoun. Yet another war broke out between the Scots and the English, a war in which duties were weapons and staple trades the casualties. It was merely intensified by the Queen's yielding her assent to the Bill of Security. The situation was fantastic and intolerable for both sides. Union had become a pressing need. The fears of the Scots, and particularly the Presbyterians, for their independence had to be set against the desperate need for a share of economic prosperity in a country which had been denied such prosperity ever since the time of Wallace by the trouble which now raised its head again. Nor did federation provide the solution: it could not settle the succession. Repeal by the English Parliament of an act which rendered Scotsmen aliens went far to create a favourable atmosphere. A Commission met in 1706. The representatives of the Scottish Estates in no way represented the people of Scotland or the English proposal of forty-five Scottish members in a British House of Commons, as Rait contends, might never have been agreed. It is no great advance on the number conceded by Cromwell as a dictator and conqueror. Here the lag in parliamentary evolution in Scotland proved a sore menace to true independence, if it prevented an open breakdown in the negotiations. But the promise of a new era in trade lured the Scottish Commissioners, while the assured independence of the Kirk by a special Security Act set at rest the greatest fear in the minds not only of the General Assembly but of the people. Scottish law remained independent also. A sum of £398,085 10s. was to compensate Scotland for the Darien disaster—an interesting admission—and for her share-to-be in the burden of the National Debt. And there was the comforting knowledge that Parliament could interfere in Scottish affairs only at a distance of four hundred weary miles. The nobility found pleasure in the proposal for closure of their number, which would protect their ranks from *parvenus*; but only sixteen of their number were to sit in the British House of Lords. On 16th January, 1707, the Treaty of Union was passed by the Scottish Estates.

A bedlam of popular opposition to the Union arose in Scotland, and anger increased over one-sided benefits of the Treaty, a good example of which is the Toleration Act of 1710, protecting Episcopalians in Scotland at a time when

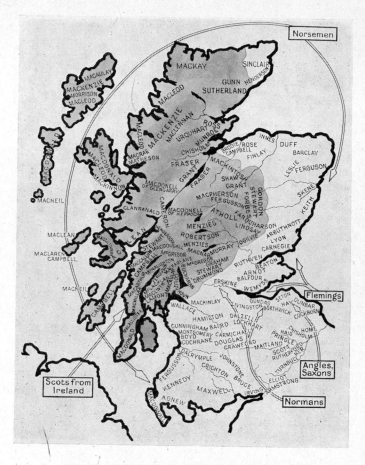

SCOTLAND: CLANS AND FAMILIES

(*Note:* The names included are only a proportion of the total.)

Presbyterians in England were being loaded with new difficulties. If the Jacobite rising of 1715 caused Presbyterian Scotland to side with the English Whigs against the Tories and the Highlanders, it ended by encouraging national feeling in Scotland through Lowland sympathy with the Highland prisoners of the Government, and the seeds were sown of a romantic tradition for all Scotland by the omission of the Clan MacGregor from the Act of Pardon. Still no trade benefits of the Union had become apparent, and feeling constantly ran high, fostered by incidents the greatest of which was the Porteous Riot of 1736. Captain Porteous had ordered soldiers to fire on a mob in Edinburgh which had shown sympathy for a condemned smuggler. He was tried, condemned, and reprieved; but the mob avenged itself by lynching him, and when Parliament tried to punish the city of Edinburgh with penalties and indignities, Scotland found vent for her feelings in a united opposition. But when the second Jacobite uprising took place, with the coming of Prince Charles Edward in 1745, only a very few Scots, most of them Highlanders, supported the Stewart cause. The Lowlands were preoccupied with thoughts of commercial development, and resented the disturbance. But Prince Charles came at a moment when Britain was engaged in a Continental war, and he and his Highlanders descended upon Edinburgh and defeated Cope at Prestonpans before any strong force could be concentrated against him. There was some mild elation: a stirring, at least in those Scots who came in contact with the Prince, of certain ancient loyalties which had never been awakened by the Hanoverians. But the Prince was a Roman Catholic, and the almost equally ancient fear for their religion, coupled with their new hopes for prosperity, held the Lowlanders back, and only 300 out of the 10,000 hoped for joined the Jacobite standard at Edinburgh. Even so, the Prince might have succeeded. Had he pressed his march from Derby, London must have fallen as Edinburgh had done, at least leaving the issue in doubt; but instead, the long retreat began which ended in the defeat of a disheartened Stewart army at Culloden.

The present Highland problem is a direct result of the repressive measures which followed Culloden. The reason for Highland turbulence had been feudalism, which developed on the basis of the clan system long after it had died elsewhere, and which bound each clan to its chief in a loyalty to the death given in return for the land held of him. Primitive as it might be, this system maintained the necessary sociological and economic equipoise. Government action after 1746 'solved' the problem of Highland intransigeance simply by throwing out this balance. Sheriffs-substitute took the place of hereditary jurisdiction by the chiefs; the chiefs were converted into landlords, to be paid in rent instead of services; the tartans and panoply which had been the symbols of the Highland social system were proscribed. That the system had become intolerable is undeniable, but the only remedy was a slow adjustment as the Maori way of life eventually became adjusted to the British way in New Zealand. The chiefs, as Dr. Johnson found, came to 'expect more rent, as they have less homage'. In many regions, the greed of the former head of the clan drove his people to emigrate, as through the generations the decay was to be hastened by the sheep-farm and deer forest clearances. The simple rhythms of the clan existence were destroyed by the pen as they could never have been by the sword.

Very different was the result of the 'Forty-five' on the Lowlands. The last lingering danger to Presbyterianism had been banished, and the fierce energies of the Lowland Scot were at last free to experiment with industry and commerce, even to plunge into the strange delights of culture. Politics had never been an interest of the Scots, who had found their politics in religion and had in any case been too busy fighting for their freedoms. Before the rising, the King's ministers had been well content to leave Scottish affairs in the hands of the Duke of Argyll. The electorate numbered a few thousands, and in the burghs corruption was notorious. But the force which rendered constitutional reform inevitable was the massive concentration of great thinkers in Edinburgh, Aberdeen, and Glasgow: men who were acknowledged intellectual leaders not in Scotland only, but throughout Western Europe. The status of such men as Hume among philosophers, Robertson among historians, Adam Smith among economists, Thomas Reid among divines, and Lord Kames among jurists contrasted with the lag in the methods of government, and increasing pressure for reform culminated in the work of Henry Dundas, Viscount Melville. There was widespread sympathy

for the Revolution in France at first; then, as its success became
a threat, reaction set in and maintained itself until the end of
the Napoleonic wars. The Industrial Revolution gave new
momentum to the movement for reform. Success opened with
the Scottish Reform Act of 1832, which produced a mere eight
new burgh members, and not until 1885 was the Scottish
representation increased to seventy-two. But the Act of 1832
ended the election of burgh members by Town Councils
and handed it to householders paying annual rent of £10,
while in the counties the figure was £50. As notable a result
as any, however, of the struggle for reform was the development
of a political party spirit in a country hitherto innocent of it.
Early Tory ascendancy gave place to the triumphant supremacy
of the Whigs which carried reform, and this in turn became
the great tradition of Scottish Liberalism. This was far from
being a mere transference of English party sentiments to
Scotland: it reflected the aggressive independence of the
Lowlander, took its inspiration—as already stated—from a
remarkable group of great minds, and derived its energy from
a determination to develop commercially for the first time
Scotland's natural resources. Robust as the political growth
of Scotland might be, however, it implied no real attempt to
combat the injustices and disadvantages inherited from the
Union, and there can be no pretence that Scotland possessed
anything approaching equality of status in affairs of government. Scottish affairs were the concern of no one in particular
of Cabinet rank. A Secretary for Scotland was not appointed
till 1885; and not until 1926 did this office become one of a
Secretaryship of State. It is to the Kirk that we must look
for evidence of the great traditional fighting spirit which
would never admit defeat in the face of any odds. By mid-
eighteenth century, the fierce flame of Calvinism appeared to
have been quenched in a flood of Moderatism, which scorned
the extreme faith of the Covenanters and ridiculed it, earning
itself approbation at the time, and indeed in the opinions of
most writers since, by coming to terms with worldly affairs
in general and providing an intellectualism which the Kirk
of Knox had always lacked. The fundamental honesty and
grandeur of the old faith had been obscured. But it was not
dead. The issue of State encroachment upon things of the
spirit, that old challenge to Andrew Melville's 'Kingdome of

Christ', suddenly breathed into it a new and magnificent vigour. Moderatism had long compromised with Caesar by submitting to the Patronage Act of Queen Anne, whereby a Presbytery must accept the nomination of a minister presented to it by the parish, which in effect meant the landowners. In 1833, the General Assembly, under the leadership of Dr. Thomas Chalmers, accepted this for the challenge it was. The Court of Session, supported by the House of Lords, upheld the Act: but in 1841 the Assembly deposed seven ministers elected in accordance with the Act, and the Parliament paid no attention to a petition addressed to it; so, on 18th May, 1843, a body of more than four hundred ministers walked out of the Assembly and, under the Moderatorship of Chalmers, founded the Free Church of Scotland. The four hundred sacrificed their livings and their manses for the Knoxian principle that the things of the spirit are independent of the State, and their courage should be a matter of pride to their countrymen in these times.

This fighting independence on the part of the Kirk was in the ancient tradition; so was the acceptance of the disadvantages of the Union settlement by Scots politicians throughout the nineteenth century. The Kirk had always been the representative democratic institution, and Parliament had counted for little for so long that the seriousness for Scottish affairs resulting from the minority Scottish representation in the joint Parliament took many generations to disturb the peace of mind of the common man in Scotland. Not that the Scots urge to defend rights and fight for independence passed politics by, but it entered into the broader political issues of the United Kingdom as a whole. It gave force to the great Radical movement in the early part of the century when again many Scots sought martyrdom for their principles—this time the principles of parliamentary reform and extension of the franchise. *The Scotsman* arose in 1817 as organ of this movement. Twenty years later the same fighting spirit found vent in the Chartist movement. The Radicals were satisfied at last only by Disraeli's Act of 1868. This restless jealousy for the rights of man appeared also in the Trade Union movement, powerful at an early stage in Scotland and a strong influence towards parliamentary reform, and some of the greatest of the Union leaders, such as John Burns and Keir Hardie, were of the ancient Lowland fighting stock. Never, however, did the Scots reformers make Scots affairs a plank of their platform. Not until the waning prosperity of Scotland in the twentieth century forced itself upon everyone's attention in the north did the cause of Scotland as a nation re-enter Scottish thought at all. Not until after 1920 did it find even the faintest reflection in politics. In the period since, it is important to distinguish between Nationalism, with a capital N, and a broad but almost imperceptible tendency of thought and feeling much less extreme yet much more solid which transcends party politics. For example, Scottish members at Westminster, once lost in a vast English majority, have latterly tended to draw apart upon certain issues. The parties have considered the question seriously. In 1924, the Scottish Liberal Association drew up a resolution in favour of a Scottish parliament for Scottish affairs, and in the same year the Duke of Montrose evolved a scheme for the devolution of Scottish affairs into Scottish hands. Labour opinion expressed itself in the same vein, as in Mr. George Buchanan's proposal in 1924 for a constituent assembly. The factors which brought about this remarkable unanimity will become apparent in the pages which follow. They may be summarized by saying there was general agreement that the decline in the common weal of the country could not be remedied in a legislature which could only devote a handful of days in the year to discussion of Scottish affairs. Even so, it is doubtful if the man in the street has taken much interest in the question. The Scot is a stubbornly unpolitical animal. It can be taken as fairly certain that, of average Scots, nine out of ten are unaware of the difference between the purely separatist National party and the moderate party known as Scottish Convention which hived off from it in 1942. It is doubtful if one in ten realizes how wholeheartedly his legislators of all parties are agreed upon the need for a new attitude to Scottish affairs. The proportion of Englishmen prominent in the nationalist movements in Scotland surely has a special significance.

CHAPTER V

DISTINCTIVE INSTITUTIONS

SCOTLAND is reputed to have emerged from history with her key institutions intact, and distinctively Scottish. Substantially this is true, although it is easy to lay too much emphasis on the contrast with the same institutions in England, and it must be remembered that two centuries of close contact with England have worn away some of the more uncompromising points of difference. I will outline here briefly the present forms of the principal institutions: the Church, the Law, the Schools and Universities.

The Established Church, the State Church in Scotland, is the Church of Scotland. The essential difference between the services in England and in Scotland is that in the first country the service is one of worship, whereas in the second the preaching of the Word takes first importance. In Scotland, ritual has been simplified so far as is consistent with reasonable dignity. The absence of what might be termed a 'professional finish' in the service sometimes jars upon the eye and ear accustomed to the mellow and well-practised formalism of even quite small churches in the south. In an important Scottish city church, such as St. Giles's in Edinburgh, more attention is paid to the pattern of the service; but as a general rule it may be taken that ritual and music are always subordinated to sermon and prayer. Instrumental music was long frowned upon, and it is only seventy or eighty years since the organ found acceptance. The singing of the congregation was traditionally led by a precentor with a tuning fork. In some remoter parishes there is still opposition to instrumental music and to the great body of vesper hymns and anthems which have been incorporated from the music of other churches, and experience of a humble country service lacking such advantages may leave one with doubts about the unreasonableness of that attitude. The sermon is no longer the lengthy and formidable exhortation or denunciation of past times; but it is still the core of the service, still the matter by which the earnest church-goer decides whether his morning on a hard, pine pew has been truly well-spent or no. It is still the subject

54

IV. CEREMONY

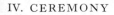

LYON KING AND KNIGHTS OF
THE THISTLE (*Scottish Pictorial Press*)

MODERATOR OF THE CHURCH
OF SCOTLAND (*The Scotsman*)

MEMBERS OF THE COLLEGE OF
JUSTICE (*Scottish Pictorial Press*)

of vigorous criticism. The minister himself is deeply respected, but not as a being apart. He is not of a priestly caste, but rather a representative of the congregation—he is indeed elected, 'called' to his charge by the kirk session and approved after trial by the congregation itself. He is not appointed by higher authority, because there is no higher authority to appoint him in a church in which all men are equal, and when the ministers gather in Edinburgh in May for the annual General Assembly of the Church they go there in a sense as spiritual delegates of the people. The General Assembly is the supreme court of the Church, and it is presided over not by the Lord High Commissioner, who is simply the formal representative of the King, but by an elected Moderator. The Moderator, although he may represent the Church on occasions of State and so rank in precedence with the head of the State Church in England, is in the Assembly *primus inter pares*. Between the kirk session and the supreme court of the Assembly there are other courts: the court of the presbytery and, higher in the scale, the synod. But all are cogs in a jealously democratic system, and a layman elder is just as much entitled as any minister to be sent as delegate to any of the courts, even to the Assembly itself.

The organization and significance of the Presbyterian Church have perhaps never been better defined than by Principal Rainy in the series of three brilliant—I had almost said racy— lectures which he delivered in 1872 as a counterblast to lectures given by Dean Stanley on the Church of Scotland. 'Presbyterianism', said Rainy, 'meant organized life, regulated distribution of forces, graduated recognition of gifts, freedom to discuss, authority to control, agency to administer. Presbyterianism meant a system by which the convictions and conscience of the Church could constantly be applied, by appropriate organs, to her current affairs. Presbyterianism meant a system by which quickening influence, experienced anywhere in the Church, could be turned into effective force, and transmitted to fortify the whole society. Presbyterianism meant a system in which every one, first of all the common man, had his recognized place, his defined position, his ascertained and guarded privileges, his responsibilities inculcated and enforced, felt himself a part of the great unity, with a right to care for its welfare, and to guard its integrity. From the broad base of the believing people the sap rose through Sessions, Presbyteries, Synods to the Assembly, and thence descending diffused knowledge, influence, organic unity through the whole system. Yes, Presbyterianism is a system for a free people that love a regulated, a self-regulating freedom; for a people independent, yet patient, considerate, trusting much to the processes of discussion and consultation, and more to the promised aid of a much-forgiving and a watchful Lord. It is a system for strong Churches—Churches that are not afraid to let their matters see the light of day—to let their weakest parts and their worst defects be canvassed before men all that they may be mended.'

The Church of Scotland has something like one and a quarter million members. The small minority which dissented from the Union of 1929 has maintained itself apart as the United Free Church (Continuing). Its structure is similar to the Established Church's; its General Assemblies are held alternately in Edinburgh and Glasgow. Outside the establishment, most of the churches south of the Border are represented with the exception of the Anglican itself. The near equivalent to this last in structure and ritual is the Episcopal Church of Scotland, but it is an independent body. Although the number of its communicants is only a little more than 60,000, they tend perhaps naturally to be drawn from a landed and influential stratum of society. The Roman Catholic Church counts almost half as many members as the Church of Scotland, widely spread but proportionately most dense probably in the strongly Irish basin of the Clyde and in parts of the north-west Highlands where it has survived the Reformation yet maintains amicable relations with the extreme Presbyterians who are its neighbours.

By Articles 18 and 19 of the Treaty of Union, Scotland retained her own legal system. With the passage of time, there has come to be a great deal of ground common to both English and Scottish systems. Substantially, for example, the mercantile law of the two countries is the same; and again, although procedure is different, the criminal laws are similar north and south of the Border. Also, the fact that the House of Lords became the ultimate court of appeal for Scottish cases has had its effect, although it should be realized that House of Lords

E

decisions in Scottish appeals may also be binding in English courts. Fundamentally, however, the Scottish system has remained distinct from the English.

The essential difference between the two legal systems is one of outlook. The English lawyer has always preferred to build up his corpus of law from decisions made in actual cases, so that English law became by accretion a vast complex of precedents; whereas the Scottish lawyer, with a clear set of principles in his mind, evolved his law logically as a machine to put those principles into practice. Nothing could better illustrate the reasoning of the two peoples, and how it diverges. The Englishman, rather than anticipate a difficulty, relies on his native common sense to extricate him when the difficulty arises, whereas the Scot prefers to devise a system beforehand. It is a commonplace statement that Scots law is substantially Roman law, but it is untrue, for Scots law is as unique in its way as English. At one time the English and Scottish systems were alike and the history of the divergence is lost, for the Scottish records were removed by Edward I when he took the Stone of Destiny and unfortunately were more easily mislaid. A reasonable explanation has been given by Lord Normand in his presidential address to the Holdsworth Club of Birmingham in 1941. After the reign of Alexander III, war, poverty, and domestic trouble not only divided the two peoples but largely destroyed the Scottish legal institutions and hindered the rise of new ones. The lay sheriffs would base their decisions on their own ideas of justice and equity, without reference to legal technicalities. Then came the period of foreign influence, the great formative period. Scots students were debarred by war from attending Oxford and went instead to Bologna, Paris, Leyden, especially the last. There they learned a certain amount of Canon Law, but as time went by a great deal more of the Civil Law which, throughout western Europe, was based on the principles of Roman law. James I, deeply imbued with English ideas after his long captivity, tried hard to establish English law in his kingdom but failed; and when the Court of Session had its foundation early in the sixteenth century, the model for it was the Parlement of Paris or possibly the College of Justice at Pavia, and it left no room for any other parallel court. The result was the single, rational system which so markedly contrasts with the dual, amorphous, perplexing

English system and its parallel developments of common law and equity. Indeed, the coherency of Scots law is a tribute to the legislative capacity of the much-abused Parliament of Scotland.

The law of persons and the land law are the features in the Scots system which differ most from the English. The notoriety of Gretna weddings has led to the impression that marriage is a casual affair in the north, but the simplicity of the principle underlying the contract by mutual consent of the parties in no way renders the contract the less binding. The equality of the contracting parties has always been recognized by Scots law, whether in divorce proceedings or in the rights of succession, where either spouse has a legal claim to one-half of the other's movable estate. In the matter of the land-tenure system there is a clear illustration of the coherency and logic of Scots law. As in other western European countries, the shape of the feudal structure of military tenure has been retained, although transferred to a commercial basis. The ancient system is commemorated even in the term 'feu' itself, which is held by 'vassal' from 'superior', and the feu should be carefully distinguished from the English lease, for the vassal remains in undisturbed possession of his land till doomsday so long as he makes his payments and so fulfils his part of the contract. Titles to land are secured from accident or any possibility of interference by the device of requiring that all deeds concerned with land tenure or its transference must, in the form of a copy, be deposited in the Register of Sasines, which is kept in the Register House in Edinburgh, where they are open to public inspection.

The supreme courts in Scotland are the High Court of Justiciary and the Court of Session. The first administers criminal law and is presided over by a judge sitting with a jury of fifteen. The second is the chief civil court of the country. It meets always in the Parliament House of Edinburgh, and consists of an Inner and an Outer House. In the Outer House are the five judges of first instance, the Lords Ordinary. The Inner House consists of two courts of appeal, with the Lord President head of the first—and of the Court as a whole— and the Lord Justice Clerk head of the second. In the interest of expediting the law there is much flexibility, and a Lord Ordinary may sit in the Inner House in order to make the quorum of three, as a judge of the Inner House may sit in the Outer. Cases may be heard by courts of seven or even of the entire thirteen judges, but after the latter instance there can be no re-consideration except by the House of Lords. Criminal prosecutions are in the hands of officers of the Crown, the chief of whom is the Lord Advocate. Such prosecutions are simple and straightforward: the criminal is safeguarded from the prejudicial publicity which may arise from magisterial examination, for he has one trial only. The verdict is taken upon a majority vote, and in case of reasonable doubt it may be brought in as 'Not proven'.

Below the Court of Session and the High Court is a peculiarly Scottish institution, the Sheriff-Court, a local court which sits in all towns of considerable size. It is more ancient and more significant than the County Court in England, for not only has it criminal jurisdiction but there is no limit to the value of the case which may be brought in it. The Sheriff presiding, or the Sheriff-Substitute, may try any case arising in his sheriffdom provided in criminal cases the due sentence is not greater than two years' imprisonment. Sheriffs are appointed almost invariably from members of the Scots Bar, rarely from among solicitors. Great confidence is placed in the Sheriff-Court by litigants and comparatively seldom are appeals taken to the much more costly Court of Session. The prosecuting officer is a State official known as a procurator-fiscal. Below the Sheriff-Court, justice is administered in minor offences by several varieties of lesser court, chief among them the Burgh or Police Court.

The Scottish Bar does not offer prizes comparable to those of the English Bar, yet at the same time it is more costly and difficult to become a member of the Faculty of Advocates than to belong to the General Council of the Bar. Parliament Hall in Edinburgh bears many resemblances to some particularly exclusive club, hidden away behind the colonnades of a grey courtyard where the wheels of traffic are hushed. On a winter afternoon, when the fires in the great fireplaces glint on the parquetry, the interloper who must pass this way to the National Library among the wigged figures strolling with their clients feels he has penetrated where he should not. The entry fees for the Faculty total about £500, and there are long, briefless years for the young Advocate to face when he is not permitted even to 'devil' for more fortunate members of his profession. Nor are the ultimate goals of the successful Advocate remunerative as similar posts in England are. The salary of a Sheriff-Substitute is £1,100 to £1,750, which counts as full-time remuneration and debars the officer from private practice. The Lord President of the Court of Session receives £5,000 a year, the Lord Justice Clerk £4,800, the other judges £3,600. But there is a certain atmosphere and prestige about the Parliament House, which maintains a trickle of recruits, even from among qualified members of the English Bar. The lawyers of Edinburgh are likewise closely organized. The two bodies through the members of which most legal business is transacted are the Society of Writers to the Signet and the Solicitors to the Supreme Court. The first body is the older and its designation of 'writer' is the characteristic Scottish term for a lawyer. In some of the more austere streets and squares of the New Town of Edinburgh, every third or fourth doorplate bears the device 'W.S.' or 'S.S.C.', and although law-agents of other towns and cities have the right to take their business direct to the Supreme Court, in practice most of them put their business through the Edinburgh firms.

The subject of Scottish education is delicate ground. There is a tradition that it is better than English education and, thanks to Knox and his aim of a school in every parish, there is no doubt for a long time it had a substantial lead; but the lead has been wiped out, and many things in the present system are under criticism.

The overwhelming majority of children in Scotland attend the State schools, still generally known as the 'Board' schools, which are divided into primary and secondary. Every parent is obliged to give his child an elementary education between the ages of 5 and 14. By the Education (Scotland) Act of 1918 education authorities were set up for every 'scheduled burgh' and county, and 'public' schools were transferred to their jurisdiction. The Act safeguards the spiritual interest of any church or denominational body which may have managed the school before 1918. Even quite small villages possess their elementary schools, but the thinly populated areas of the west and north-west present a problem which sometimes calls for the placing of a resident teacher in a remote farm. In some remoter corners and in certain of the islands, no secondary school is within reach, and a child may have to board in the nearest town where such a school is to be found. There is a uniform curriculum, wide in scope and containing provision for many special subjects such as domestic science, engineering, and music, and close attention is paid to physical training, including organized games, an activity which has been developed out of all recognition in the past twenty years; but the standard to which all school work is directed is that of the Leaving Certificate Examination, roughly equivalent to the Preliminary Examination for the Scottish Universities. In spite of standardization, there is individuality as between schools: some have earned themselves notable reputations. And there has recently been a remarkably enlightened policy in school architecture, with close attention given to light and air and to the amenities of setting and interior decoration, in which some of the foremost young architects and painters have been given opportunities. Then, independent of State aid, there are several famous endowed day schools. Edinburgh is particularly rich in these, from the ancient George Heriot's Hospital to the Merchant Company Schools—George Watson's school for boys and girls, Daniel Stewart's College for boys and Edinburgh Ladies' College. There are several celebrated day schools of the grammar-school type: the Edinburgh Academy, Glasgow and Kelvinside Academies, Aberdeen Grammar School, the first three at least given a considerable English bias by their habit of picking staff with Oxford or Cambridge degrees—and blues. True public schools in the English sense are few: Fettes College and Loretto, and Trinity College, Glenalmond, the last governed by the Episcopal Church.

The age-old tradition that the 'lad o' pairts', the boy with natural ability, should have the opportunity, no matter how poor his circumstances, to make his way and obtain a University education dominated the school curriculum for many generations. For a long time this has had excellent results: the way to the laurels of the M.A. was open, but it was hard and demanded perseverance and character which safeguarded the system from abuse. Every one knows the story—a true one— of the Highland porter who, in reply to the idle curiosity of the bishop as to what his sons were employed on, said that one was a well-known divine, another a judge and the third a Cabinet Minister. Now, thanks to the Carnegie Fund, the way is easier. Whether this is a good thing has recently been called in question with some bluntness by a prominent Scot, and for some weeks a storm of controversy raged in the columns of the newspapers. On the one hand were those who maintained that the Scottish tradition was on true democratic lines, and they had many excellent results to put forward to prove their case. On the other hand the critics claimed that what might have been a liberal education and training in citizenship had become a preparation for examinations which many would never have to face. Curricula have indeed been 'liberalized' out of all recognition, but the goal of a University education for his sons is probably still in the mind of every second Scot. And probably most of us would observe with misgivings a change in this attitude. There are regrets in some quarters—not all extreme Nationalist—that the bias in history and literature teaching is not more pronouncedly Scottish. The critics would have English history supplement Scottish, instead of the reverse, now generally true. The same critics deplore that the literatures of the Gael and of the makars are not taught at all and would like to see Duncan Ban Macintyre take the place of Thomas Gray and Dunbar supplant Chaucer.

The Universities are four: St. Andrews (founded 1411), Glasgow (1450), Aberdeen (1494), and Edinburgh (1582). Each is headed by a Chancellor, elected for life, and by a Lord Rector, chosen by the students generally from among the distinguished men of the day. The Vice-Chancellor, or Principal, is a Crown appointment, except at Edinburgh, where the Chancellor makes the appointment. High administrative policy is decided upon by the University Court, while the general conduct of University studies and affairs is the concern of the Senatus Academicus—the Principal and professoriate. A Dean administers the domestic affairs of each Faculty, and the Faculties consist of Arts, Science, Divinity, Law, and Medicine. Those limbs have not developed equally. Edinburgh, for example, is famed chiefly for its School of Medicine, perhaps the greatest in the world, and its scientific bent is apparent again in a young but already famous Department of Animal Genetics. Glasgow, with the tradition of Kelvin, is

strongly scientific. Aberdeen, a smaller University, has produced a disproportionate number of its country's younger
writers. Although St. Andrews, and to a lesser extent Aberdeen, bear slight superficial resemblances to Oxford and
Cambridge, the teaching methods of all the Universities are
radically different from those of the great English pair. Instead of the system of individual tuition in separate colleges,
lectures for the ordinary degree course are delivered by the
professors or lecturers to classes sometimes of several hundred students, and only at St. Andrews and, elsewhere, in
the honours degree course are tutorial methods usual. Again
with the partial exception of St. Andrews, none of the Universities is residential in the Oxford sense. The student
finds his own lodgings and is subject to no academic discipline
outside the precincts of the University. Corporate social life
is still sparse, and must needs be while students' lodgings
are scattered over a great city, but the Unions, both men's
and women's, have grown in importance, and the number of
hostels is increasing and will increase further, thanks to the
munificence of such benefactors as Sir Donald Pollock in
Edinburgh. But the cloistered intellectualism of Oxford has
not, and can never have, a strong appeal for the youth of a
people with a long tradition of urgent purpose, a tradition
more than ever likely to be kept alive to-day.

On the other hand, on the academic side, there is much
valid criticism of the neglect of the humanities. The Scottish
Universities for a long time have tended to become training
colleges. Carnegie scholars in their hundreds pour through
to graduate M.A. or B.Sc. and presently return as teachers
to the communities they came from, their minds unwidened,
undeepened, unmatured by intellectual experience. The
faculties of Medicine, of Law and even of Divinity also suffer
from this vocational narrowing-down of the horizons of learning, while the close association with the Universities of such
professions as engineering and accountancy adds its weight to
the constricting influences. The bias tends to be all towards
science, and towards applied science at that. There is too little
opportunity for higher research work, and those graduates
who aim at such work, time and again perforce drift to Oxford
or Cambridge, which attract a generous proportion of the best
minds from the Scottish Universities. To a great extent this

must be attributed to comparatively meagre endowments in the north. An average student at a Scottish University is not in a position to forego the earning of his living for a few years, and many Scots to-day, especially among those who have seen conditions in other countries, are disturbed at what seems to them to be the failure of the Universities to play their part in developing constructive thought.

CHAPTER VI

THE PROBLEM TO-DAY

SCOTLAND to-day is characterized by a medley of hopes and fears which are perhaps better understood by the peoples of the European states than they are by the people south of the Border. She is, in a way, a test case. Her problem is the problem of whether the nation is a unit to be discarded as of merely sentimental interest or a germinal organism without which human society cannot maintain itself in a sound condition. The tendency in the British islands between the two wars has been consistently in the direction of centralization. London more and more had become the heart of affairs. The more threatening economic and political conditions became, the more the national resources shrank in upon London, and the weaker grew the limbs and body of the country. Scotland, conjoined to England, felt she had for long been no more than one of the limbs. Naturally, in that condition, she was one of the first areas to suffer the shrivelling process. Every home Scot remembers numerous instances of firms and factories which suffered by the contraction, with employees flung on the labour market without chance of re-employment. Very early the Scottish railway companies were absorbed by two great companies centred upon London. The Scottish banks became tied to the English banks. Multiple stores sent their tentacles from the south and took over great and respected shops in the Scottish cities, blunting further the individuality of the north with the monotony of standardized goods and service, as the cinema had already blunted it. Only the more foolish and fiery regarded this as a piece of deliberate victimization of the Scots by the English. It took effect within England also. The disease was not even confined to Britain. Obviously, its deadliness was greater in Britain, because the vigour and resistance of the various components of the nation were most unequal. A fatal ending, sooner or later, seemed inevitable, not for one or two of the four peoples only, but for all. It became clear that some form of devolution had to come. The outbreak of war supplied the impulse, and one shrivelled limb after another became injected with the old life and vigour and hope as the circulation of employment and prosperity and well-being was restored.

Scotland shared in the new life, vigour, and hope; but she remained a limb. No guarantee existed that she would not fall victim to a more devastating attack than ever of the old disease, and she seemed to have no power to influence what happened to her. Thought in Scotland in these two or three war years has turned as it had not turned for two centuries to weighing the pros and cons of her relationship with England. There had been a noisy but inconsiderable Nationalist movement for many years, in its extreme form clamouring for complete separation, but it may be said to have passed its peak when it descended into the arena of party politics, becoming merely one among many small groups in futile opposition to the weighty machines of the great parties. But the new national consciousness now stirring is something altogether greater. Partly, I think, it owes its inspiration to a rebirth of belief in nationhood within the British Commonwealth since the triumph of the Battle of Britain and the refusal to yield of one small nation after another even when crushed by that satanic apotheosis of centralized power, Hitlerism. More immediately it is inspired by a series of domestic problems which have grown so great that the need to tackle them on a national scale cuts across all considerations of party or creed.

The problems are really many aspects of one great problem: it can be seen in the figure of something like 1,500,000 people out of 5,000,000 dependent on unemployment relief as recently as three years before the war; it can be read in the Glasgow infant mortality rate of 87 per thousand in 1938 as compared with Chicago's 34 or Amsterdam's 31; it is apparent in the chronic shortage of houses in Scotland now estimated at 500,000—the percentage of overcrowding is almost six times that of the figure for England and Wales; it is evident in the increase in the adverse trade balance from £2,000,000 in 1913 to £22,000,000 in 1937. And although the facts and figures are not there to back it up, there is the same significance in the relaxation of the hold of the Kirk, and in the absence of a virile school of thought, a vigorous culture or a richly characteristic way of life among the people. It is with this composite problem, and with the impact upon it of the new consciousness of the need for plan and effort, that the remainder of this book is concerned.

CHAPTER VII

THE COMMON WEAL

A N epoch-making debate in the House of Commons on 12th May, 1942, was opened by the Secretary of State for Scotland with a citation of unemployment figures showing that between 1931 and 1936 almost a quarter of the insured workers in Scotland were unemployed. He reminded the House that from 1921 to 1931 Scotland lost by emigration 80 per thousand of her population, as compared with 5 per thousand in the case of England. The figures are grim, but the realities behind them were grimmer still. Scotland at a juncture not so long before the present war was a nation very nearly derelict, collapsing so fast that it seemed incapable of doing anything to save itself. Three-fifths of the people were crowded into the narrow industrial belt from Forth to Clyde, and the basic industries which had brought them there were slowing to a standstill. The social consequences were tragic.

Living conditions were almost unbelievable in the poorer quarters of some cities; 22·6 per cent. of Scottish houses were overcrowded, as compared with 3·8 per cent. in England and Wales. This was a cumulative legacy from the last war. It implies conditions so primitive that attempts to advance the standard of civilization in the country as a whole were as irrelevant as attempts to teach table manners to a man dying of starvation. Entire families slept not merely in one room, but in one bed, and a single water-closet had to serve the half-dozen families living in a tenement house, while the sub-letting of rooms at high rents is an accompanying evil still rife in certain places. The last census revealed that 44 per cent. of the population occupied houses of one or two rooms. The standard of health naturally has been gravely affected, and children, especially very young children, are the first to suffer by such conditions. Infantile mortality before the last war was lower in Scotland than south of the Border—substantially lower; but although there has been a steady improvement in the Scottish figure, its relation to the English figure has been reversed, and when it is set beside the statistics for New Zealand or Holland the comparison is deeply disquieting. New Zealand and the Netherlands show respectively 31 and 38 deaths per thousand births, as against 80 in Scotland. The figures are for 1937. The causes of death are infectious and respiratory diseases and other ailments traceable to the environment into which the babies are born, and the first month of life, the most dangerous time, is the period which has shown fewest signs of betterment.

Great headway has of course been made against the serious scourges which accompanied bad living conditions in former times, and even the danger of tuberculosis has been got largely under control. Among adults in Scotland, it is not actual disease which gives concern so much as a widespread short-coming in fitness in men and women in the prime of life. The Report of the Committee on Scottish Health Services published in 1936 drew special attention to the sickness and defects revealed by the medical inspection of school children, the sickness returns for the insured population and the army recruiting figures. Sixteen per cent. of Glasgow school children were stated to have ailments which could not be ranked as minor, 20 per cent. of the insured population to be incapacitated for work, and 38 per cent. of potential recruits rejected on medical grounds. And this took no account of mere subnormal health or minor defects. 'The vital statistics of Scotland', states the Report, 'are disquietingly less favourable than those of England and Wales and several other European countries.' That is the picture eight years ago. In 1938 there were 417,000 separate cases of incapacity, a number which represents twenty-six million wasted days, and it has been found that

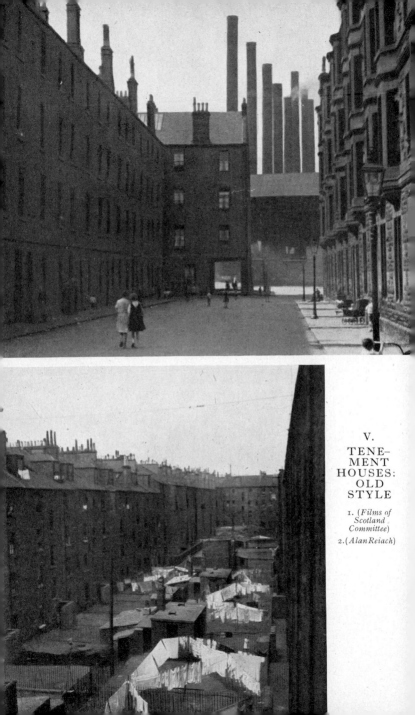

V.
TENE-
MENT
HOUSES:
OLD
STYLE

1. (*Films of Scotland Committee*)

2. (*Alan Reiach*)

nearly half those cases were persons of less than middle age. The significance of this in a small country requiring every ounce of vigour and initiative in the fight for existence is apparent.

Nutrition statistics show the same picture from another angle. The war against actual malnutrition has been going well for two generations, but under-nutrition is much more difficult to combat. An Advisory Committee reported in 1935 that the average milk consumption in Scotland was less than half a pint per day, although it should be seven-eighths of a pint, that it was 'very probable' that insufficient fruit and vegetables were eaten, and that some of the sugar and highly-milled cereals in the diet should be replaced by potatoes. The Scottish Health Services' Report states that 'the practice in the homes of the people is not abreast of modern knowledge of nutrition'. This is true not only of the cities. In the Highlands and Islands the standard of nutrition is one of the most serious obstacles to rehabilitation. The Report states that most of the witnesses examined 'deplored the passing of the old staple foods of porridge, salt herring and potatoes and the substitution of shop bread, tinned foods, tea and sweets, and other goods purchased from shops or, more commonly, the traders' vans'. More recently, Dr. Fraser Darling has repeatedly called attention to this. Light has also been thrown on the poor standard of cooking in the north and west. Bad cooking has become more and more characteristic of Scotland in general since the staple foods were departed from or were processed and commercialized, as oatmeal has been, and most of the virtues taken out of them to render them less strange to vitiated palates. The preparation of vegetables in particular is little understood. Among working-class families green vegetables are either over-cooked or they are not used at all. The excess of starches and carbohydrates in the Scots diet of to-day must be equally injurious. 'High tea' is the traditional Scottish evening meal, and a healthy meal it was when it included such items as fresh herring or kippers, eggs, oatmeal bannocks, fresh butter, home-made jam and a girdle scone to finish with. But replace those foods by fish and chips, canned meats and pickles, new bread and bakers' scones and cakes, as the last generation has done, and you have the key to the digestive troubles which undermine the health of so large a section of the Scottish community. Poverty, of course, has dictated the diet in the overcrowded areas; a mother is only too glad to feed slabs of doughy bread to her children if it fills their stomachs. The unemployment which scourged industrial Scotland before the rearmament programme began dragged down the trend of nutrition—a state of affairs which the balanced diet of war-time canteen feeding has thrown into sharp relief by the excellence of its results.

The weight of this social problem, this millstone, is perhaps most apparent of all in mental and moral effects. The gang-wars of the Glasgow slums have received wide publicity for many years, but they are no more than the local symptom of an ill to which all Scotland has been subject. 'Overcrowding and slums', writes Professor Mackintosh of Glasgow University, 'interfere with sleep, create friction between individuals, and poison the springs of family life. Under such conditions education is beating her wings in vain, because every outlet for intelligence—work and play—is continually obstructed.' The many forms of delinquency among the youth of the country are most concentrated in those areas which have for so long been notorious for their overcrowded condition. Such delinquency is of course also the legacy of long years of unemployment, for many children were born to men who had never known what it meant to receive wages and as the number of the children increased in the family the allowances received were inevitably greater than any wage the man could possibly earn in employment, and the vicious condition was perpetuated. Indifference, enervation, absence of initiative and even positive vices followed, until thousands of the most able and conscientious craftsmen in the world became demoralized and sullen. The wonder is that so little trouble did indeed emerge out of so much hopelessness, and that so many hundreds of thousands retained the will and the capacity to place derelict industries on their feet again as happened under the threat of the present war. Not even the most enlightened piece of planning to-day offers so much hope for the future of Scotland as that resumption of effort by her workers.

So much for the problem—the dark side of the picture. There is much to set against it. The most important thing is impossible to assess: the awakening of what appears to be a real national consciousness, as opposed to mere dilettante nationalism, with signs of rousing hope, enterprise and determination. It owes a great deal to the stimulus of war. But many practical measures have been taken. They will achieve greater and greater success as the weight of popular resolution is thrown in behind them.

It has been stated above that much headway has been made against the more serious scourges. Scotland's work has not been more notable than the work of other countries, but the world campaign against tuberculosis was in certain aspects led by Sir Robert Philip who, nearly sixty years ago, planned and put in operation in Edinburgh a scheme co-ordinating sanatoria, clinics, and home visiting. He realized at once that the incidence of the disease depended upon living conditions. Largely as a result of his pioneering, and in spite of adverse conditions in the industrial areas, the death-rate from the disease in Scotland fell from 354 per 100,000 in 1871–80 to 69 in 1938. Dirt diseases such as cholera and various fevers have been eliminated by improved sanitation—an achievement probably greater in Scottish than in English cities, for the 1936 Report quotes a medical opinion of a century ago, that the Scottish mortality from such diseases was then 'far above the level of corresponding towns in England or on the Continent'. It must be remembered that in, for example, the Old Town of Edinburgh there are houses of the sixteenth and seventeenth centuries still in occupation, and they have been retrieved from slumdom without recourse to the housebreaker. But the problem of unfitness is a much more elusive one. It demands a war not of extermination but of prevention. The ground has been well mapped by such investigations as produced the 1936 Report, which is a masterly document. A great deal of encouraging reconnaissance has been carried out, and a certain number of major advances achieved. Children's health has been improved beyond recognition. In twenty years rickets among Glasgow school-children has been reduced from 9 to 1·2 per cent., and on the positive side there is a steady increase in height and weight, substantial credit for which must go to free milk distribution and to the recognition of the value of sun and fresh air among those responsible for schools. War-time conditions have assuredly increased the pace of the advance through the elaboration of

VI. MODERN BUILDINGS

1. COLLIERY BATHS, COMRIE, FIFE (*The Fife Coal Company Limited*)

F   2. THE WEIR PARAGON (PREFABRICATED) HOUSE (*G. & J. Weir Limited*)

nursery and nursery-school schemes due to the enormous
influx of women to industry. War-time strain has also induced
a big-scale experiment in the possibility of anticipating
incapacity and breakdowns in health. It has been conducted
in the Clyde Valley, the most industrialized region in the
country, and it involves the co-operation of panel-doctors
in a campaign of preventive medicine to head off serious
disabilities at the stage of mere unfitness. This is in line with
suggestions in the 1936 Report. Another recommendation
of the Report has been fulfilled under war conditions by the
conversion of the huge luxury hotel at Gleneagles into a
rehabilitation centre for miners. It is vital there should be
no subsequent retreat from those first positions gained.

The most longstanding—and perhaps the most outstanding
—scheme to defeat ill-health in Scotland is the Highlands and
Islands Medical Scheme, responsible for more than half the
area of the country but for only one-seventeenth of the population. It dates from 1913. The circumstances which brought
it about were the difficult communications, poverty and
ignorance of hygiene, the threat of physical deterioration
through defective diet, and the burden of the rates in an area
where an added sixpence in the pound may bring in no more
than £40. Grants are paid to doctors to enable them to attend
patients for a uniform fee irrespective of how far they have to
travel, so that no place is without the services of a doctor at a
reasonable fee. In practice, the scheme has come to attract
doctors of much greater ability—young men of energy but, it
may be, without the capital to start elsewhere. Everything is
done to encourage these men, even to making post-graduate
courses of study available. Subsidies are given also to local
nursing associations: they have raised the standard and
numbers of nurses substantially. Surgeons and specialist
services are also subsidized, and hospitals, ambulances and
telephonic and telegraphic communications come within the
orbit of the scheme. An air ambulance brings cases to a city
hospital in an hour or two. The breadth of the conception
and the efficiency and sympathy of its execution are object-
lessons for the future.

Housing is the root-problem in raising the common weal of
Scotland—housing not only in the sense of accommodation
but of environment also. It begins as a question of building

and ends as one of education. A century of vicious over-crowding has effects which cannot be eradicated by brick and trowel alone. However, the physical aspect is the urgent one It has been estimated that 500,000 houses are required, although in the years between the two wars nearly 300,000 working-class houses were erected, giving homes to a quarter of the population. As Dr. Bowie points out, the obstacle has been the shortage of skilled labour and of materials in the building trade. Only a modest total could in the years before the war be erected annually—enough perhaps to cope with the normal increase in the demand but not to make substantial inroads into the accumulating deficit. It is recognized that only a resolute and gigantic attack on this problem, co-ordin-ating a special development of the building industry to deal with the demolition of unfit property and its replacement, on the one hand, and the social aspect on the other, will serve to house the country as it must be housed. The new houses must satisfy not only hygienic standards: they must be so designed and built that the heritage of a pernicious slum-outlook be defeated, which implies not merely space and gardens but the creation of a new sort of community spirit to supplant the old. For many years this was not understood by the hard-headed Scot—if, indeed, it was understood any-where in Britain—and the result has been the soulless crusts of shoddy and planless dwellings which encase so many historic and lovely towns in Scotland, Edinburgh among them. But this phase would seem to have ended. Only here and there have better things been done as yet—war and threat of war before it blighted much; but the war has brought unexpected activity in planning on a grand scale, involving some of the country's most enlightened young architects. These men have studied closely the spirit behind domestic housing in other small northern countries such as Sweden, Denmark, and Holland, where slums and drabness are abhorred as fully as bad sanitation. They are also alive to the need to comply with the needs of the practical housewife, and her evidence has been taken. The local authorities too have inaugurated far-reaching schemes, from the establishment of satellite towns, as at Kincorth, near Aberdeen, to the open discussion of the need for replanning entire cities in which Edinburgh has been engaging. The more the problem is approached in a spirit

of eager anticipation, the more quickly will the ultimate
objective of the whole health and housing campaign—the
injection of hope and confidence into the people of Scotland—
be attained.

CHAPTER VIII

THE WEALTH OF THE NATION

FOR more than a hundred years the fortunes of Scotland
have hung mainly upon her heavy industries. The twin
resources which spelled prosperity during the Industrial
Revolution were iron and coal, and one small region of
Scotland possesses them side by side, with the great additional
advantage of easy access to the sea. Moreover, iron and steel-
working have a peculiar appeal for the temperament of the
Lowland Scot. His sense of craftsmanship and his powers of
creation had been frustrated for a very long period by endless
wars of many sorts which had eaten into his soul, and his
energies were ready for a craft of heroic proportions, demanding
fighting qualities. In the challenge of the Iron and Steel Age,
the Scot discovered his talent—it might even be said his genius
—for devising mechanical things. Kipling linked it with an
aesthetic urge. It embraces all Scots, Highland as well as
Lowland, and sometimes I think it may not be going too far
to trace in it an outlet for the ancient Celtic instinct which
produced endless ingenious and rhythmic patterns. Anyhow,
in a few generations, Scotland drained itself of population
towards the basin of the Clyde and the neighbouring coal and
iron deposits. Most of the small region was turned to black
desolation; but out of that desolation poured a steady traffic
of ships and machines, larger and larger, and in themselves
more and more beautiful as the years went by.

The iron industry in Scotland dates from 1759, when the
Carron Works were founded at Falkirk. Thirty years before,
the denuding of English forests had sent iron-smelters north-
ward in search of sources of charcoal, but it was not Scottish
iron which they used. The Carron Works were built upon
the ironstone of the great Lowland carboniferous belt. At
this time coal was fast replacing charcoal as the smelting fuel,

and there were rich coalfields in the vicinity of the new works. For half-a-century the Scottish iron industry laboured under difficulties, as the coking quality of Scottish coal was lower than English coal's and as much as 25 per cent. lower than Welsh, so that the Scots required at least twelve tons of materials to produce one ton of pig-iron. Two momentous discoveries revolutionized the industry. David Mushet proved the high grade of ore in blackband ironstone—hitherto despised although present in immense quantities in the Lowland belt; and in 1828 Neilson invented the hot-blast furnace, which simplified the smelting of blackband. Blackband possessed the additional advantage of containing coal in association with the ore. It became possible to produce three times as much iron for every ton of coal. The key to Scotland's mineral resources had been found.

It was a key which unlocked the door to long-denied wealth, for iron was the philosopher's stone of the nineteenth century. Each stroke of fortune seemed to lead to another. The export of pig-iron demanded shipping. The new ships required steam engines, and Glasgow had the materials and the skill to make them. When the new industry of building iron ships arose, the iron was there and a river into which to launch the ships. Railway transport demanded the same materials and similar forms of skill. An immense ganglion of related industries grew up in the basin of the Clyde—so immense and so stable that when, about 1880, much of the local ore became exhausted, the industries continued to expand upon imported ores. Coal, too, found new markets in the lighting of factories and cities, and the huge export of coal again enhanced the railway and shipping industries. Indeed, the great shipbuilding tradition of the Clyde was born only from the union of the coal and iron industries, for Aberdeen held the supremacy in wooden ships. Bell's *Comet* was the portent of change. Within fifty years the iron fleets of Glasgow had beaten the clipper-ships of Aberdeen, and when mild steel was introduced as hull material, the metallurgical resources of the Clyde put that river far ahead of all its rivals. The iron and steel industries and the engineering and shipbuilding industries were united to form a single economic colossus, armed with skill and enterprise and capital which seemed to render it invincible.

Scotland as a nation was behind this colossus. By far the

greater part of her skill and organization were committed to the heavy industries. One-third of her population was directly concerned in it. This relative importance of one group of industries is the vital fact in Scotland's economic position to-day, because from the intensity of her concentration upon it arise not only the problem of her future prosperity, but the problems also of her social welfare, and even to an extent of her culture. The great industries of the Clyde basin and of the industrial belt were dependent entirely upon the export trade, and Scottish capital as well as English poured out into undeveloped lands overseas together with manufactured goods, and handsome profits returned to be invested in a further expansion of the industries which had created the capital. The last war brought this epoch of lending to a stop and trade slowed down. Other countries learned how to build their own ships and locomotives and engineering works and bridges, and then erected tariff walls to protect their developing enterprises. A rapid decline in the demand for heavy goods set in as steam was superseded as a power-agent by the internal combustion engine and by electricity. Steel and iron yielded place to light alloys of great strength. Material commitments in the shape of plant and capital, as well as the fierce momentum which the Scot gathers when he has set his mind on doing something, made it difficult to turn aside into other paths as more adaptable centres such as Birmingham or Coventry were able to do. The shipyards of the Clyde, as well as the heavy engineering shops of Glasgow and Lanarkshire became liabilities. Thousands of skilled pairs of hands at the street-corners of Clydebank and Renfrew and Coatbridge thrust deeper into threadbare pockets while a new economy arose in the outer world, beyond their ken—an economy in which technical skill was used to produce an immense number of everyday things such as vacuum-cleaners and radio-sets. Those things were produced cheaply, replaced often. The marketing of them created a vast new field of employment, as profits came to depend less and less on sheer quality and more on enterprise in advertising and selling and speedy delivery. At first thought, it may seem incomprehensible that Scotsmen, who invented the telephone and television and did much of the pioneer work in radio, should not be able to exploit what they had done to give their country a share in the profits.

VII.
CLYDE-
BANK.

R.M.S. QUEEN
ELIZABETH ON
THE STOCKS AT
JOHN BROWN'S
SHIPYARD

(E.N.A.)

The chief explanation is that the heavy-industry commitment had been so immense that only a planned and vigorously-promoted reorganization on a national scale could save the situation. It demanded co-operation and discipline. The Scot—particularly in his own country—is a 'thrawn' individualist. He takes a pride in being unco-operative, and tends to regard any central authority either as a potential tyrant or as an Aunt Sally, instead of identifying himself with it and attempting to modify it in accordance with his way of thinking. That he identifies the central authority with London may partly explain this. But in the absence of any resolute attempt to mend the national economy, the situation prior to the war was black.

War has wrenched the decline to a stop. It has set the steel mills going as never before, as it has set the song of the riveters echoing again across the narrow waters of the river from the Broomielaw to the Cart; but it is recognized to be a false stimulus, as it commits the country more and more deeply to just those heavy industries which brought about the crisis before. As Dr. Bowie, the distinguished economist who is Principal of the Dundee School of Economics, has put it: 'When disarmament comes along we shall find we have been giving blood-transfusions not to the young industries on which our future must ultimately depend, but to the anaemic old industries that were already doddering down the hill.' Happily this would appear to be realized in Scotland to-day. In responsible circles there is keen concern about the future, and it was for this reason that the Council of Industry was set up in 1942. The Council has no executive powers, but it collects data and advises the Council of ex-Secretaries of State upon certain tendencies, let us say, which may be prejudicial or beneficial to Scottish industry, and the case is presented in the proper quarter. If there is complacency in Scotland about the economic future, much of it is popular complacency, for even yet there is no sober realization, outside the most heavily industrialized areas, of the dangers which faced the country and which will face her again in, it may be, a more intensified form.

Lesser Scottish industries are numerous, interesting and in some instances unique, but with a very few exceptions they are not of a sort which can ever exert an influence on the general prosperity of the country. They tend to cater for limited markets. An example is printing, which is the chief industry of Edinburgh. There is something of the medieval guild spirit in the Edinburgh printing trade, which is as much concerned with its good name and the quality of what it does as with the marketing of its goods. There is a further similarity in the care with which apprentices are selected and trained. For many years past, each boy has had to pass rigid tests, medical, psychological, and educational, while there is a three-year course of study at a printing school, for which the boy is released for an entire day each week without loss of wages. The trade is a very highly paid one. An ancillary industry in the Edinburgh district is paper-making, and again high quality is the aim, for the bulk of the esparto papers produced in Britain comes from the district. Similarly, one of the greatest printing-ink factories in Britain has its works in Leith, with its offices in a delightful old seventeenth-century house over-looking the Forth. It is a creditable sign that this group of old industries maintains its traditions and its health. At the same time, it is all too easy to sentimentalize over them unduly, when the burning need is for cruder and more robust young enterprises capable of unlimited expansion. It is less well-known that Edinburgh also possesses electrical engineering works of the first importance—is it significant that they played an important part in the electrification of the Southern Railway, although Scotland itself possesses not a mile of electrified line?—and that she has some of the largest rubber mills in the country. Aberdeen, Dundee, and even some of the small east-coast towns likewise possess manufactures capable in time of absorbing large numbers of workers. Small matter as it may seem now, all this is of the first importance for the future, because a more equitable distribution of industry and popula-tion is even more vital for Scotland than it is for Great Britain as a whole. Brewing is an industry of the south-east which has steadily added to its prosperity, and Edinburgh is the second-largest centre in the kingdom. The whisky distilleries occupy a still more important place in the economy of the north-east. Neither beer nor whisky can contribute substan-tially towards employment, but they may give considerable encouragement to agriculture and to subsidiary industries such as bottle-making and coopering: Neil Gunn has pointed out that whether or no he gets a market for his barley makes all the difference between solvency and insolvency to the farmer in the north.

Textile manufactures have always had a place of special importance in Scottish economy, and here again the trend is towards quality before quantity. Almost every part of the country produces some characteristic fabric of its own. Woollen manufacture is a national industry in Scotland to an extraordinary degree. It spreads into every corner of the country and even into the homes of the people, in which it contrasts with the more localized English industry. Only in the crofting districts is the wool used to any extent now the product of the local sheep, for it is in the nature of the Scottish industry that it can utilize all sorts and varieties of wool. The basic distinction between Scottish woollens and English worsteds is that in making the worsted yarn the wool is combed, a process which removes all but the longer fibres, while the woollen yarn undergoes the carding process, which tangles all the fibres together. The carding process permits the Scottish industry to employ everything from the coarsest home-grown material to the softest and most luxurious Kashmirs and vicunas. Mills around Elgin and the north-east have specialized in luxury goods woven from Chinese camels' wools or Peruvian vicuna; the great Border industry has grown up through the manufacture of fine, plain cloths derived largely from the sheep-rearing country surrounding the mills; Aberdeen evolved such materials as 'Lindsey Woolsey', with a linen warp and a woollen weft. The home of the Harris Tweed is the crofting country, and particularly the Outer Isles, where the fleece of the hill-sheep is spun in the cottages and coloured with the lovely plant-dyes the recipes for which have been handed down through the generations. Essentially the Scottish woollen industry in all its branches is a luxury industry. But it is a luxury industry in the best sense. Not only does the carding process produce a texture with the high insulating qualities necessary for a severe climate, but the siting even of the larger mills in some of the loveliest parts of Scotland has had an indisputable effect on the aesthetic aspect of woollen manufacture. The wide and subtle ranges of colour in the Scottish landscape are reflected in the blending of colours in the cloths, while the texture of

VIII. THE LAND

1. ABANDONED HIGHLAND CROFT (*Robert M. Adam*)
2. HARVESTING NEAR EDINBURGH (*The Scotsman*)

the carded yarn makes possible a natural depth and mystery of tone which contrasts with the harsh artificiality in mass-produced cloths. This essential high level of quality ensures a prosperity for the Scottish woollen industry even in the face of the formidable large-scale textile industries south of the Border, and the manufacturers are by no means insensitive to changing fashions and maintain close contact with the dress-designers of London, Paris, and New York. Unfortunately, the crofting area has not the same advantages, although Highland Home Industries Ltd. has done its best to market their tweeds to advantage. Materials of far inferior quality have flooded their markets under the name of 'Harris Tweeds', in spite of the authorization of a trade-mark by the Board of Trade in 1934, and it is essential both to the crofter and to the buyer that means be found to ensure that the fine, individual product of the Highland cottage is protected against unscrupulous competition by the machine-made article.

The other Scottish textile industries are hardly recognizable remnants of industries which once had their roots in Scottish soil. Chief among them are the jute mills of Dundee and Angus, the linens of Dunfermline, the thread mills of Paisley, and the lace manufacture of Ayrshire. To these might be added the linoleum works of Kirkcaldy, in Fife. The jute mills, which draw their raw material from India, and which link Dundee and Calcutta in a curiously close relationship to their mutual benefit, were an adaptation of the dying linen industry, the chief of all Scottish industries in the eighteenth century. Linen manufacture at its height was as widely national as the woollen industry to-day. Spinning, weaving, and bleaching were carried on in every parish, and flax was a universal crop even in the days of the run-rig system, although conditions for its cultivation were far from favourable. For a long time the products of Scottish looms were coarse, and suffered in competition with the fine fabrics of the Continent; but the industry received generous encouragement from the State, and spinners were imported, who have left odd traces of their coming in such place-names as Picardy-place in Edinburgh. The agricultural revolution drove out flax as a home-grown crop, and great quantities were imported from abroad. Before long Glasgow and Paisley were making fine lawns and cambrics which found a market even in France itself, but the chief market was America, and the War of Independence dealt as hardly with the exports of linen as it did with the vast tobacco trade of Glasgow. However, the skill was there, and in the west the capital also. The enterprising mill-owners of the west saw their opportunity of maintaining and augmenting their fortunes in the cotton industry which the power-looms of Lancashire were so largely wresting from India. The machinery of the mills of Glasgow and Paisley, powered largely by fast-flowing streams, was about 1780 switched over to cotton-weaving, first by combining a cotton weft with a linen warp. Skill in weaving fine linens pre-determined the trend of the new manufacture—to its ultimate downfall. Muslins rivalling the most delicate output of Indian looms were in production by the end of the century and Paisley specialized in shawls with a pattern based on the 'pine-cone' *motif* of India with such success that every woman in the early years of the nineteenth century aspired to a collection of them. Huge fortunes were made. But this prosperity depended on the fickle turn of fashion, whereas the mills of Lancashire concentrated on fustians and such plain goods, and in a few years the cotton industry began to surrender its skill, capital, and enterprise to the advancing heavy industries.

Perhaps the first essential for a return to prosperity in Scotland is the establishment of a mass of light industries, easily adaptable, to meet the new markets, which are so largely domestic and subject to mood and fashion and the wiles of the advertising profession. Scotland's products have been arresting and dramatic—Cunarders and great bridges; or they have ministered to the tastes of the small group of the well-to-do—whisky and fine woollens. A proportion of them must come down to the humdrum level of pots and pans, radios and cheap cars, and supply the man in the street with what he needs or fancies. There lies the permanent demand. It is widely hoped that the recession of the armament programme will leave behind the nuclei of the right sort of new industries—plant, for instance, capable of producing on a large scale the internal combustion engine of which Scotland has so long unaccountably fought shy. But a new awareness and enterprise and willingness to risk capital on the chance of big results is needed. And there is a parallel need to learn the business of marketing. Anyone who has visited the Scottish

SCOTLAND: POLITICAL

sections of exhibitions either in London or abroad knows the embarrassing *naïveté* of their balmoralistic approach. Few Scottish businesses possess the machinery to sell their goods furth of their own country, although this fault has frequently been pointed out. Of this Dr. Bowie remarks: 'Most Scottish industries continue to lose business through sticking to nineteenth-century selling methods which they find it difficult to abandon because they are neither grouped in large amalgamated units, nor do they develop the effective co-operative organizations, either of which would enable them to establish powerful centralized selling units.'

Agriculture is proportionately more important to Scotland than it is to England. Its importance is not lessened by the fact that in a little over a century the number of agricultural workers has fallen to about one-seventh, because the output per man is vastly greater. Only one-fifth of the population now lives outside the towns. Scottish agriculture predominantly consists of stock-farming, as might be expected in a country with wide areas of soil too thin to yield grain crops. Aberdeen, Angus, and Kincardine are the principal meat-producing regions, the home of the famous black Aberdeen-Angus breed of cattle. A great dairy-farming industry is centred in the mild meadows of Ayrshire and Galloway. The sheep-farms of the Borders exist primarily to supply the woollen mills of their own valleys. The rich arable farms lie in the Lothians, in Fife and in Angus, which can show some of the best-managed agricultural land in the world.

It is less than two hundred years since the possibilities of the Lowland farm-lands were discovered. They were badly drained and primitive methods of cultivation were in use until well into the eighteenth century. The climate was harsh, and it was accepted that only the poorest sorts of grain, such as grey oats, were hardy enough to withstand it. The amount of corn got from a plot was little more than the amount sowed in it. There was none but makeshift fodder for wintering the cattle, which in any event were of the poorest breeds. But the greatest obstacle to the development of the land was the ancient 'Celtic' field-system, known also as the 'run-rig', which contrasted very unfavourably with the three-field system in operation in England. Under this ancient system the farm-land consisted of an in-field, nearest the steading, and an out-field beyond. Manure from the byres and stables was lavished on the in-field, and a constant succession of oats and barley was cultivated, sometimes with the variation of peas, beans, rye or a little wheat, until the ground was totally exhausted, when it was left to recover. Only about one-tenth of the field could be cultivated at a time. The out-field was sown with corn for a year or two, and then for several years left under grass on which the stock and horses grazed. Further, not one farmer, but a number of tenants worked the farm. Each field was divided into 'riggs', or ridges, and for these the tenants drew lots annually; so that enterprise and improvement were impossible, and the communal labour entailed led to constant confusion.

The agricultural revolution of the nineteenth century brought about an astonishing reversal of those conditions. Here again, as in the Industrial Revolution, the redoubtable determination and energy of the Lowland Scot came into play. A tangle of prejudices had to be cut through—prejudices against tree-planting, against the enclosure of property by fences, against new crops, against new methods of cultivation and farm-machines. But enlightened landowners and farmers set in motion a change which ended before the century was out in the pupil, Scotland, changing places with the teacher, England. All this has been maintained: the acre-yield in Scotland is still higher than in England, and in comparison with other parts of the world is higher still.

There is still, as Mr. James A. A. Porteous has pointed out, an immense area of marginal land to be developed. On the hill-pastures, the spread of bracken demands a well-worth-while expenditure of energy and money, and to keep the new-won pastures in condition there must be a part-reversion to cattle on the hills—which again demands expenditure. Certain districts of Scotland, too, are unmatched for the cultivation of soft fruits, but the full potentialities of this have never been realized. The Blairgowrie area has been developed, but there are parts of Tayside where the deer have invaded former orchards. In the Clyde Valley, strawberry fields and orchards are giving way to acres of tomato-houses, which would seem to be a pity, for the soft-fruit crops of this sheltered, fertile valley have for generations been of the highest quality obtainable, and blossom-time from Lanark down to Crossford and beyond is still one of the few pieces of gentler loveliness in Scots scenery. On the other hand, there are considerable soft-fruit possibilities in the Western Isles. Mr. Porteous notes that in 1939 strawberries ripened outdoors before the end of May in Islay—and there is one spot at least more than a hundred miles to the north where apricots are reputed to have grown in former times. Communications are the chief deterrent to the development of a trade in early fruit and vegetables in the islands.

It is one of the anomalies that Scotland, under-nourished as her people have been, and notably neglectful of vegetables, has nevertheless maintained her place in the forefront of agricultural research. The best-known centre of this work is the institute at Bucksburn, near Aberdeen, named after the late Dr. John Quiller Rowett. Its field is the study of nutrition, animal and human. Since 1930, the Imperial Bureau of Animal Nutrition has been centred at the Rowett Institute. Laboratory research is given practical tests at the Duthie Experimental Stock Farm, a branch of the Institute run on business lines, where there are facilities for large-scale experiments in feeding livestock of all kinds. Through the Imperial Bureau, information is made available to agriculturalists throughout the world, and Scottish farmers are by no means neglectful of the advantages which the Institute offers them. The success of the experiment in providing milk for children through the schools is due to the Institute, which has other equally important dietetic campaigns under way. A particularly able team of scientists, with Sir John Orr at its head, has won the Rowett its reputation in the short space of twenty-five years. Parallel to the Rowett is the Scottish Soil Research Institute known after its founder as the Macaulay Institute, at Craigiebuckler, also in Aberdeenshire, counterpart to the Rothamsted station in England. Among its most interesting work is the research carried on in Lanarkshire and in Lewis into the possibilities of improving peat soils, and it has been found that for an outlay of a few pounds per acre land able to support a mere dozen sheep can be made to feed 120, as well as 35 cattle, 200 poultry and a pig or two. The North of Scotland College of Agriculture at Craibstone and the West of Scotland College have been doing equally valuable work for a longer time, and the first is notable as the only school in the kingdom for farm women. Pioneering work has been done also in the production of clean milk, while the Lothians can show some remarkable experiments in market gardening, where by intensive manuring, soil sterilization and the outdoor use of heat as many as seven crops have been taken in a single season.

Grave problems, however, face Scottish agriculture after the war—not on the technical, but on the economic side. As in industry, for war needs there has been encouragement of products which have no natural market in peace. There must be concentration of enterprise, capital, and effort on products which Scotland is best fitted to produce and best placed to market.

Romantic misconceptions are perhaps responsible for the common belief that Scotland is a country of great forests but the reverse is true. Hardly a tree was to be seen in the Lowlands early in the eighteenth century, and although this has been remedied in so far as agriculture and industry permit, the great forest areas of the Highlands were disastrously denuded during the war of 1914–18 and the depression which followed permitted of little re-afforestation except by the Forestry Commission, which had planted 126,000 acres before the end of 1938. The chief indigenous tree of the Highlands is the Scots Pine. Numerous sorts of foreign conifer, however, such as Douglas Fir and Norway Spruce, flourish splendidly, and in the West Highlands the warm, damp winds encourage a respectable growth, even in such trees as the Californian Redwood. The planting of forests would alter for the better the entire economic life of the Highlands. The principal obstacles are the acid nature of the soil, especially in the west, and the compression of the glacial drift soils in the glens; but draining and deep ploughing can overcome them. It is esti-mated that the forest area of the Highlands could be increased five times without taking in any ground which might be suitable for grazing. It may be too much to expect a wood-pulp industry to result, in opposition to the Canadian and Swedish industries with their inexhaustible resources; but Highland forests might well supply the raw materials for cellulose and plastic substances required by new aircraft or motor-car industries in the Lowland belt.

Off the Scottish coasts is some of the best sea-fishing in the world. Herring has always been part of the Scot's staple diet. The fleets follow the shoals round the coast, beginning early in summer in west coast waters and working round to the North Sea fishing grounds. In the Firth of Clyde—where the celebrated Loch Fyne fleets operate—the season continues all the year. White fish of the highest quality—cod, haddock, whiting, plaice, sole—are plentiful in Scottish waters, and Scottish boats concentrate on bringing them fresh to market. The salmon of the estuaries of the Solway and the Tay and of some of the deep western inlets of the sea are unequalled. The lobsters of the Hebrides and crabs of the east coast—the 'partens'—are also of high quality. Indeed, it is notable how Providence has compensated Scotland for her hard conditions by blessing her with sea and land harvests succulent far above like harvests anywhere else; and it is a reflection on modern tastes that she should have suffered by it. The demand, as Mr. Peter F. Anson states in his little book on the sea-fisheries of Scotland, is all for coarse, cheap fish to serve the innumerable chip-shops. As a result, the number of Scottish fishermen between the two wars declined by almost half. Ports which a few decades ago numbered their vessels by hundreds are now almost derelict, with only a few boats alongside their quays. A few vessels as a rule comprise a fleet in Scotland, whereas the English companies own many of modern sea-going type which can fish the distant deep-sea grounds and bring in their catch frozen, meeting the demand for quantity and securing profits which enable them to maintain the finest of equipment. Many of the Scottish boats are out-of-date. The Highland crofter-fisherman in turn suffers by competition with the greater resouices of the large ports of his own country. Many of the fishermen, Highland and otherwise, live their lives through burdened by debts. This plight has been matched by a loss of continental markets in the years before the war which can be illustrated vividly in the drop in Russian requirements from 70,000 barrels in 1934 to 10,000 barrels in 1936, and at the best there is an uncertainty which makes their trade an anxious business to men who have no capital to fall back upon.

Like agriculture, the fisheries are proportionately of far greater importance to Scotland than to England. In relation to populations, Mr. Anson gives the proportions as seven to one. It is therefore vital for Scotland that her fisheries be restored to prosperity, and the quality of her fish would seem to argue that the advantage would not be hers alone. In pre-war days one heard constant complaints in Scotland about the increasing inability to obtain fresh fish of the first quality, and horror was frequently expressed over the 'dumping' of herring in the sea because they failed to secure the minimum price laid down by the Herring Industry Board. But the indignation found no outlet in systematic and sustained pressure to compel the righting of the situation by decisive action —an all too-common weakness of Scottish popular opinion in recent times. There was nothing irretrievable in the situation. Reorganization of the industry on a collective basis was recognized to be essential, perhaps also its concentration in a smaller number of ports and—here, as in other spheres of Scottish industry—planning on a large scale of new markets and development of the old. It was essential too that the industry itself should learn co-operation on the Norwegian model, that capital should be forthcoming for new boats and equipment. The most acute difficulties faced the herring fisheries. The recommendations of the Herring Industry Committee include schemes for grants and loans for boats, for the chartering of boats from the Board by fishermen, for the defeat of the recurrent surpluses and shortages by extensive cold storage. Overseas markets are to be encouraged, to which end the possibilities of dehydrating and freezing, kippering and canning are to be investigated. The home market is to be stimulated by delivery of herring of best quality in the best condition. The high nutritive value of the herring should be an added stimulus towards the carrying out of those recommendations.

The Highlands are a self-contained problem, because their fate is the fate of the Highlander; and as the Highlander is by temperament a pastoralist, it would seem that any solution of the Highland problem must have as its mainspring the land. This is, perhaps, self-evident; but it should be remembered that a large body of opinion still looks on the tourist trade or even on sport as affording perfectly possible solutions or at least major part-solutions. The Highlands are by no means the least part of Scotland's agricultural resources. Their past history is, briefly, this. After centuries of feuds and cattle-stealing, by about 1700 an important stock-breeding industry had been established on the high pastures, and the sturdy strain of black cattle was marketed to English dealers—the tale of the drove-roads is a Scottish parallel to the tale of the cattlemen of the Far West. After the middle of the century, the Highland landlords discovered the greater money-making possibilities of large sheep-farms, and the small tenants who had reared the black cattle were driven out to make room for the sheep. Intense hardship was caused, and the great exodus of the Gael to America and to the towns began; while at the same time the link between man and soil was broken, and the land—never, certainly, much developed—fell into neglect at a time when the farm-lands of the Lowlands were beginning to respond to intensified cultivation. Sheep-farming pros-pered. The produce of the Highlands increased in value about ten times. But the profits were barren profits so far as the Highlands were concerned. Then, in the post-war depression after the downfall of Napoleon, the sheep in turn were driven out and the area of deer-forest vastly increased, as the landlords found that to rent their moors to the wealthy not only brought them a surer profit, but involved them in almost no outlay at all. Again the man who paid was the humble Highlander, and a renewed exodus took place, while the land suffered a renewed phase of neglect and deterioration.

A vicious downward spiral was established. The people, driven out or disheartened, had no longer the power to develop their land ; and the land, neglected, became less and less able to support the people. The momentum of the spiral was evilly maintained by wars, which struck at the people—always the best of shock-troops—and at the land, in the devastation of deforest-ation. It was maintained too by changing economic conditions in the world, whereby the Highlander grew less and less able to compete for the money which became more and more essential to arrest the spiral. The resources of the Highlands would seem to be such that the basis of life must be a crofter-system : that is, a man must have several occupations—fishing, perhaps, in season, the rearing of stock for sale, participation in home industries such as tweed-manufacture, forestry, and always the production of the main foodstuffs to maintain himself and his family. The land itself is of two sorts, a large area of hill grazing and a small area of arable in strips and pockets along the coasts and in the glens. The greater part is rocky and often peaty, too acidic to tolerate most crops. The high ground has late frosts. There is little sun and a short season. To get over those difficulties is by no means impossible, because there are ample lime deposits which could sweeten the soil, while a study of crops and manures can help to counter the bad conditions; but such things cost money, and the crofter finds money difficult to make. He is far from his markets. The breeds of cattle suited to Highland conditions mature slowly, and the demand is for younger beasts and smaller joints. Fishing, as described above, has suffered disastrously. Homespun tweed-making wages a losing struggle against commercial competition, and again marketing is a serious obstacle. Afforestation is beyond the control of the crofter and, on an economic scale, beyond the means of many a landowner. But the lime is there, wanting only processing and transport. The breed of cattle can be adapted. The fish are still in the seas. The hand-made tweed has a quality of individuality unattainable by any machine. And the Gael is of a race which cannot be permitted to die out in this country, however much our loss may be another country's gain. The whole position of the Highlands is a gigantic challenge to an economic system in which wealth is looked on as a matter of possessions, to the exclusion of considerations of the common weal. We are apt to judge the Highlands backward because their economy is different from urban economy. It has become almost impossible for us to exorcise the viewpoint that sees somewhere in industrialization and business methods the route to rehabilitation, although it is a pathetically complacent viewpoint, for the cities are in as much need of rehabilitation as the Highlands. The Highlander knows bitterness; but he knows happiness too, and his pleasures do not leave a bad taste in the mouth afterwards. Above all, he is not a cog in anyone's machine. He has moments when he knows his is a good life—or could be. But he is not permitted to taste of the fullness of it because his vigour and vitality are sapped by frustration and poor nutrition—fundamentally, by the failure of his basic supports, the land and the sea. Until recently at least, his numbers have dwindled because the land and the sea could no longer support him. He has been driven from both, in part by deliberate tyrannies, but more by his near proximity to a merciless economic system against which he had no defence. He has been called lazy, but he has disproved that in many parts of the world. He will work hard, but he has the sense not to enslave himself to work just to secure wealth and position. Quite without romanticizing, he counts the smell of the pines and the sound of the burns as wealth and considers his name confers position fit for any man. But as for those pines, he must have great new forests of them to swing his axe in, and he must have the means to make his earth fruitful as well as the means to send the fish from his sea-lochs swiftly and cheaply to a market. Then, perhaps, the Highlanders may begin to flow back again to their homes from the cities they despise even if they prosper in them, for the life of the cities is no life for a pretty man and well they know it.

There are things pending which encourage one to think a revitalization of the proper life of the Highlands may not be far off. Broadly, the tendencies are all towards studying local needs rather than towards imposing general principles which may not fit those needs, and there are many scientific and sociological investigations which may come to benefit the Highlands. Among them is the work of Dr. Fraser Darling, who acts officially as adviser to the crofters on behalf of the North of Scotland College of Agriculture. He is both a biologist and a practical farmer by training; but the confidence of the crofters has been won not only by his technical qualifications, and by his sympathy, but by his epic example in making a successful croft out of seventeen acres of derelict ground on a wind-blasted island with the sole help of his wife. It is a hard life, as all life in the Highlands and Islands must be, but he is the first to admit its compensations.

The Highlands have one great natural resource hardly as yet exploited: water-power. In the Scottish Economic Committee's review, *The Highlands and Islands of Scotland*, published in 1938, there is a map on which are plotted about eighty undeveloped catchment areas in addition to areas developed or surveyed. The Cooper Committee estimated that Scotland possessed a potential capacity, counting only the important possible sources of power, of 4,000 million units.

The interest and controversy which surge around the question of Highland water-power are chiefly concerned with the application of that power, which seems a little odd to those nations blessed with an infinitely greater abundance of raw materials but with climates so much drier and landscapes so much flatter that they can muster all too little power for their needs.

The most immediate and vital question concerning Highland water-power is how best it may be used towards the rehabilitation of the Highlands themselves. There is a certain amount of natural feeling in Scotland at the thought that an area already denuded of its man-power for the benefit of industrial regions and distant countries might have its water-power also drained away to provide cheaper electricity for the north of England or even for industrial Scotland. To the business man, this feeling may seem illogical: the Highlands have infinitely more power than they could possibly absorb. But the benefits of cheaper fuel for the wheels of industry have to be weighed against the imponderable but enormously important consideration that the Highlands are the proper home of a sorely distressed element in the Scottish people. If the chief wealth of the Highlands is to be employed primarily for users other than Highlanders, then the Gael's last opportunity may slip by. It is in recognition of this that the three primary objectives of the development programme of the Committee on Hydro-Electric Development in Scotland are:

'(a) to attract to the Highlands through the offer of cheap and abundant power a share in the vital and expanding electro-chemical and electro-metallurgical industries;
'(b) to develop such further power as may be required for the consumers of existing undertakers or for consumers in its own distribution area, the surplus being exported to the grid; and
'(c) to develop on an experimental and demonstrational basis isolated schemes in isolated districts.'

The fourth recommendation of the Board, likewise, is to the effect that 'the Board should be bound to give priority to the local requirements over all other demands for their power'. The nature of those local requirements is the critical part of the problem. The Report of the Committee divides the proposals for the utilization of Highland water-power into two

SCOTLAND: INDUSTRIAL POWER

categories. By the first, the introduction of modern industries is condemned as impracticable, as the Gael is inseparable from his croft, and electric power could best be used to lighten the lot of the crofter. By the second, new industries are held to be the only hope of 'an immediate infusion of new life into the Highlands before the breaking point should be reached'. Such electro-chemical and electro-metallurgical industries as the Report suggests could very well be established even in the remoter places, and the essential improvement in communications would in itself benefit the more isolated communities, while the demand for meat, vegetable, and dairy produce would provide markets to stimulate the efforts of crofts and small farms over a wide area. It is claimed, too, that young men would no longer require to leave the Highlands to secure employment. All this is good. It must never be forgotten that the Highlands are more important than their water-power, and that in all questions of doubt the deciding factor must be the degree of benefit accruing to a region which has been distressed for two hundred years. Before all else, the immense power latent in the glens should be used to give to those glens—in so far as it is possible—the life of which they have been starved both by nature and by economic conditions. If it can be used to prepare the raw limestone to sweeten the bitter soils of the north-west, surely it should be so used, even at a formidable initial cost. Nourishment—of soil and man—is the first problem of rehabilitation. If it can be used to set up communal refrigeration plants to enable the crofter to eat his own beef and mutton, then let it be so used: the dividend will be a health and vigour which will encourage enterprise and break the vicious spiral. But based on a public enterprise though it be, such rehabilitation need not replace the Highland way of life with something new and foreign. Indeed, it must not. In one way or another, the present war has proved the fallacy of centralization. The unit natural to the Highlander is a small one, and it is by the development of more, not less, self-sufficiency in each tiny unit that success is likely to be achieved in the Highlands. The parallel of the Tennessee Valley Authority's scheme is constantly cited in relation to the Highland problem. The problem of the Tennessee Valley was over- not under-cultivation. But, in its broad aspect of the rehabilitation of a poverty-stricken and depressed region by

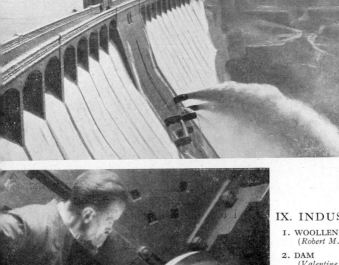

IX. INDUSTRY

1. WOOLLEN MILL
   (*Robert M. Adam*)

2. DAM
   (*Valentine, Dundee*)

3. HEAVY INDUSTRY
   (*G.B. Instructional Ltd.*)

the use of its own hydro-electric power for agricultural, domestic, and industrial development, with its careful and far-seeing attention to health, amenity, and education, the TVA programme provides an inspiring lead.

The ways in which electric power might transfuse new life into the crofting communities are innumerable. In the agricultural field, grass drying is an instance. In a wet haymaking season—there are many in the crofting areas—the grass grown loses quite half of its nutritive value, and if an efficient system of grass drying were made complementary to an intensification of grass growing the crofter would be able to keep more stock through the winter. In the home, application of electric power to cooking, lighting, and heating would conserve vital time and labour. A crofting household uses 15,000 peats per year. A good man cuts 1,000 peats a day and drying and stacking take about a month, all at a time when the labour would be better occupied on the land. From the industrial angle, power might with great profit be enlisted in the production of phosphates, calcium nitrate, and other fertilizers, the high cost of transporting which makes their price prohibitive to the crofter to-day, adding to the momentum of that vicious downward spiral.

CHAPTER IX

TRENDS IN THOUGHT

THE Golden Age in the intellectual life of Scotland is commonly accepted to be the eighteenth century, more especially the fifty years following the 'Forty-five. It is the age of David Hume and of Adam Smith, of Francis Hutcheson and of Thomas Reid, of the famed 'Scottish School' of philosophers to which Goethe and Kant in Germany and Comte in France in various ways admitted they owed a deep debt. Strangely, it is also the age in which Scotland has been least conscious of her nationhood, most abject in her relations with England, least subject to her emotions, most oblivious of the sterner issues. It was in fact an age of rarified intellectual life upon which no Scotsman can look back with unmixed pride. The fierce sense of political independence had almost wholly vanished, so that even Hume himself was at times painfully and apologetically conscious of his un-Englishness, and the equally fierce sense of religious independence had given place to that Moderatism which allowed a divine of Reid's eminence to plead with Hume for more 'atheistic' material on which to exercise his philosophical club in Aberdeen. The very name of Moderatism has an uncomplimentary sound in Scottish ears. The virtues of Scotland, like her vices, have never been moderate; and the most vital thread of thought running through Scottish history, passionate regard for liberty, is hardly glimpsed in the 'Golden Age'. That volcanic will to independence to which the Scots owed their being had been submerged. A vital fervour had gone out of Scottish thought, leaving it a prey to that tendency to speculation for its own sake which had dogged it since the day of John Major—a tendency which dogs it still. Pressing problems had developed for the Scots people since the Union. Their industries and overseas trade were bitterly penalized when they came into collision with English industries and trade, and resort to a Parliament in which Scots members were a meagre minority could have no effect. Slowly the nation began to fight back in the soundest way possible—by building up the productivity of the soil. But she was leaderless, and it was nearly the end of the century before she found another champion of her independence—Robert Burns. Burns led no movement. His was the voice of the laboriously enriched earth asserting again the liberty for which it had so long been impoverished. By his eloquence he re-established consciousness of the ancient border of Tweed and Cheviot. In no sense is his achievement a revival of the old enmity against England: it is a challenge to his own people to retain their identity and character and to assert themselves before their qualities become merged and lost. His patriotism is the reverse of jingoism. He preaches the brotherhood of man; but has the wisdom to recognize that such brotherhood can best be attained by men whose roots are deep in the earth they have sprung from. That is why his appeal is so universal to-day, even in Russia and China and other countries outside the stream of Western European thought, and why his importance to modern Scotland is so much greater than the importance of all the intellectuals of the Golden Age put together. Laying bare reality, he lit for his people the beacons of a new sort of fight for freedom.

A second tide of Moderatism submerged the Scots, notably between the two German wars. Only now are there real signs of its receding. The discipline and the evangelical fervour of the Kirk had again resumed their hold on the Scots in the nineteenth century, and for all their faults, had given direction, character, and vigour to Scottish thought. It resulted in no great thinkers. But it did more. It imbued the individuals of an entire people with a stern ideal of behaviour to maintain which they were ready to sacrifice their ordinary comforts and pleasures, and in numerous instances to undergo hardships and even death. The Covenanting spirit was reborn, and was far more widely distributed than in the seventeenth century. The advance in ethical principles may have been slight. The industrial revolution concurrently went from strength to strength upon a welter of social injustices and exploitation while even some ministers of the Kirk looked blandly on, and the 'strict principles' were often only another name for tyranny or hypocrisy. But there is no getting past the central fact that, all against the swelling torrent of a profitable materialism, an entire people so rated the independence of 'Christ's Kingdome' that they were ready to defy the State for it. Lord Cockburn considered the Disruption 'the most honourable fact for Scotland' in its history, and even the non-Presbyterian Gladstone hailed it as 'noble and heart-stirring'. It should be remembered that, under the Presbyterian system, the courageous action of the dissenting ministers in 1843 involved also their presbyteries, their kirk sessions, their congregations, and implies a depth of conviction and capacity for concerted action on the part of the people which is a pattern for all doubters of democracy. It was not only the ministers who stood to lose by it. It filled many an emigrant ship at the Broomielaw. Cargill's settlement at Dunedin owes its existence to the Disruption. And the same conviction and determination were behind the tremendous missionary movement which arose in Scotland and produced not only men like David Livingstone but the foreign mission system of the Church of Scotland which, backed only by a few hundred thousand people, has probably established itself as widely over the globe as the American missions. Agreement or otherwise with the beliefs of those ministers and those missionaries is for the moment beside the point: the important fact is the cohesion of thought and readiness to act upon it which made a little nation of five millions a force to be reckoned with and respected. And that is why the Moderatism of the twentieth century has been so damaging to Scotland.

What do I mean by twentieth-century Moderatism? I mean the readiness of the Kirk to come to terms with the world, precisely as the Moderates of two centuries ago did. Disillusionment and decline in faith were problems which faced the whole western world in 1918, but the Kirk tried to overcome dwindling membership by making concessions to youth, tried to counter the lure of cinema and dance-hall by encouraging a 'bright' social life about itself. The younger generation of writers were, and are, mostly outside the Kirk. They were restless and discontented, vaguely Nationalist, bitterly sceptical. Few had the purpose or capacity even of the lesser giants of the eighteenth century, but they joined with them in their scorn for and hate of Calvinism. Again and again there was feverish talk of a Scottish Renaissance, and bafflement at a series of miscarriages throughout the 'twenties and 'thirties always found vent in further curses upon the heritage of Calvin. Calvinism was agreed to be an alien scourge, an unnatural discipline which for four centuries had prevented the flowering of the Scottish genius; when all the while want of just such a discipline between the two wars had rendered Scotland less effective than ever in her history. Precisely as in the eighteenth century a paean went up of nostalgic longing for some exotic unfolding long denied us, while the social structure of the nation tottered under the rotting action of neglected problems of health and housing and unemployment and depopulation and the encroachments of centralized monopolies. Iron discipline was needed. The nation would have responded, as it has never failed to do. The Kirk alone could have applied it—can apply it still. That this need not mean smothering of culture will perhaps become apparent in the section which follows. But let it be said here that the reformed religion prepared the way for all the Scottish philosophers and scientists. Calvinism imposes no façade of ritual between God and Man. It recognizes God as present in all creation, recognizes in Him a divine harmony into communion with which it is the duty of every individual to strive to bring himself. The essence of Calvinist theology was, to borrow Luther's words, that 'the Bible is the cradle which contains the Word of God'; but, although they fought with the Bible in one hand, the Word of God was not the only cause for which the Covenanters died. Their allied cause, cause of all the Reformers, was the Rights of Man—the ancient Scottish cause of freedom. The Bible acquired another significance because the struggle between Rome and the Reformed Church, in its simplest terms, was the struggle of the common man against the priest to possess in his own home, in his own tongue, secure from distorted interpretation, the Word of God. That struggle won, under the Presbyterian system each Scot became in a sense priest in his own house, and the hunger arose in him to prospect for himself among the eternal mysteries. Moderatism in any form is, therefore, the enemy not only of the Kirk, but of something fundamental in the Scot. Of the old Moderates Principal Rainy in the lectures already quoted says they 'were not altogether desti-tute of some connection with religious earnestness, and they developed a striking activity in general literature. For the rest [Dean Stanley] likes the men, he likes their tone; as mental companions he gets on with them, and is at ease with them; therefore he recommends them. Did ever mortal trifle so with life questions? Was it not worth considering whether there are not, or have not been, religious forces at work here, as elsewhere, divided from Moderatism by an antagonism far deeper than the mere Scottish fervour. Was it not worth while to ask whether the decisive forces of Scottish religion can put on Moderatism . . . at any less expense than that of dying?'

The most important new movement in the Kirk to-day turns its back on the rigorously Puritan phase of Presbyterian-ism, while acknowledging the service it has done. This move-ment is led by the Rev. George F. Macleod, and its aim is a return to the spirit of the Celtic Church of Columba, which is claimed to be the model which the first Reformers strove to imitate. Dr. Macleod maintains that while Protestantism in Scotland has done much to liberate thought and to create independent, self-controlled lives it has 'lost something of an earlier genius for devotion'. He points out that the ritual of family prayers and the austerity of church services has waned, and claims that in any case the purging of the churches of all symbolism so starved the Scots people that Freemasonry and other symbol-loving brotherhoods have flourished in Scotland as nowhere else. He argues that the interpretation of the spirit of the Gospel by the Columban Church accords more nearly with the modern view that 'the Kingdom of God is among you' than does the Puritan interpretation, that Columba's Francis-like visioning of God through nature is an outlet for modern worship of the open air, that the ritual of the Celtic Church must appeal to the hunger for symbolism. The head-quarters of this movement is appropriately Iona itself, and it has drawn many young ministers to it. It might almost be called a kind of High Church movement within the Kirk. As such, it is unique and interesting.

Had I to choose a single figure as the embodiment of the Scottish intellect at its finest, there is no doubt I should take Thomas Carlyle. An hour with *Sartor Resartus* reduces to-day's babel of denunciations of Calvinism to a pitiful railing. Here in the guise of Teufelsdröckh is the mind not only of Carlyle but of the eternal Scot, burdened by awareness that knowledge of the Truth can be come at only through its own efforts, appalled by the task and filled with doubt, grimly but calmly determined, and at last triumphant. 'The Universe is not dead and demoniacal, a charnel-house with spectres; but Godlike and my Father's'. The way to this knowledge is a hard way. It demands the direst self-discipline, the sacrifice of everything to duty—to the duty which lies nearest. Not the man who follows his fancies and his pleasures, but the man who follows this path of duty to its triumphant end is the free man, the man who will share in immortality. The origins of Teufelsdröckh are far older than Knox and the Genevan Church. They lie in the cycles of retreat, defiance, and hard-won triumph of which most of Scotland's history is made up; and the rugged, uncompromising, eloquent author of *Resartus* was only one man—if a genius—out of numberless generations of men who had stumbled their ways to the same sort of con-clusions. The true genius of the Scots has often been rugged and uncompromising, never exotic although often violently

H

colourful, and as a rule it has lain dormant until the nation had special need of it. There is need of it to-day. Carlyle is the greatest, the only truly great religious thinker Scotland has produced. His contempt for democracy separates him from other philosophers among his countrymen, but who would dare say that the intolerant autocrat in him is not typical of his individualist race? And is he not the most sweeping of radicals?

The traditional political philosophy of the Scots is radical, and indeed they are all of a muscular breed that has not learned how to put aside its choler without falling into a degenerate complacency. Scots radicalism is the main driving force behind nineteenth-century Liberalism. It has always held, and still holds most strongly, that the function of government is limited and must be restrained on behalf of the freedom of the individual. Here again is something probably with ancient origins, but as a political creed it dates from the time of Adam Smith and the *Wealth of Nations* and the famous doctrine of *laissez-faire* which the industrial revolutionaries twisted into a sanction for a return to jungle law. The creed of the sanctity of the individual was purified and uplifted by John Stuart Mill who, in his essay *On Liberty*, concludes that 'a State which dwarfs its men, in order that they may be more docile instruments in its hands even for beneficial purposes, will find that with small men no great thing can really be accomplished; and that the perfection of machinery to which it has sacrificed everything, will in the end avail it nothing, for want of the vital power which, in order that the machine might work more smoothly, it has preferred to banish'. Mill has since been criticized for divorcing the State from the individuals composing it; but he may yet prove to have been wiser and more far-seeing than his critics. The truly strange fact about that century of Scottish radicalism is its extraversion: hardly ever was that searching beam turned on the affairs of Scotland herself, in spite of their sorry state, although once Gladstone himself showed his awareness by a scornful attack on the Lord Advocate for eulogizing the Union and its consequences for Scotland. This great north wind of radicalism has hardly stirred now for a generation or more. But the sky of Scotland to-day is mackerelled over with promise of a change. Radical instincts are again making themselves felt,

and it may be that a new philosophy is emerging which
Scotland is eminently fitted to work out within herself—the
creed of the sanctity of the small nation in face of the many
plans and trends which threaten engulfment.

CHAPTER X

THE CULTURAL ASPECT

S OME of Scotland's most deeply-rooted problems are
hardly to be understood at all until they are reduced to
simple terms of stone or words, of paint or music.

Except in the field of literature, Scottish culture is poor in
commentaries. There have been many catalogues of achievements, but no serious attempt to put those achievements in
perspective and assess them in terms of universal standards.
Some of the cataloguers even read as though they were making
the best of a bad job: the obvious relief with which they arrive
at a figure such as Raeburn suggests a repressed conviction
that there is no Scots genius at all. It is quite true there has
been no rich flowering, no classic period such as the Renaissance in Italy or the dynasties of T'ang and Sung in China.
High achievements have been so isolated, so apparently uncon-
nected, that they seem to be accidental . . . the ancient stone-
carvings, Burns and Carlyle, the painting of M'Taggart and
Peploe, Dunbar and Henryson and the verse of the makars,
the chaste silverwork of the late seventeenth century, the great
Gaelic poetry of Alasdair MacMhaighstir Alasdair and Duncan
Ban Macintyre. But a pattern is there for the seeking.

'The keynote of Scottish art is', wrote the late Professor
Ian C. Hannah, 'the undying tradition of the Celt.' The Celtic
is the distinctive element which distinguishes a pure Scot from
a northern Englishman, and it is natural that the distinctive
qualities in Scottish art should also flow from Celtic inspiration. Even Scots who should know better have come to regard
the Celt as a dying remnant of their race. They forget that
Gaelic was the tongue of the greater part of the area of Scotland
about a hundred years ago, and a little investigation would

show them that innumerable place-names even in the stronghold of Saxondom in Scotland, the Lothians, are of Celtic
origin. Art is a subtler test of the persistence of the strain.
The outstanding characteristic of the ancient Celtic art is its
capacity to produce endless decorative patterns, always fresh,
gay, dynamic, absolutely satisfying aesthetically, but never
except in the most highly stylized sense representational or
expressive of any intellectual ideas. It is organic and never
ceases to produce new ways of filling space, like vapours coiling and re-coiling in a flask, but always with an ordered purpose. Where there is colour, it is rich, bold, simple, and defined,
and it may be taken that colour was introduced wherever possible. The pleasure to be got from contemplation of a good
piece of Celtic decorative work, such as the patterns on the
stone slab at Nigg or on the Monymusk Reliquary—pleasure to
be got even by those with no special knowledge—is the best of all
retorts to those who believe that the expression of the aesthetic
urge through abstract forms is nonsense. Christianity of
course rapidly requisitioned Celtic art as a vehicle for its own
ends, and indeed the Picts themselves developed a remarkable
ability for representing animal forms, but Celtic characteristics
persisted and were adapted. The old instincts seemed to die
out in the later Middle Ages, only to appear again, intermit-
tently, in such media as the engraved brooches of the seventeenth and eighteenth centuries, and in the carved handles of
dirks and the engraved and inlaid brass and steel pistols of
the same period. I have been told on excellent authority that
in certain places even to-day school children have shown a
capacity and inclination to execute something in the nature of
the ancient, intricate patterns. But the Celtic genius would be
weak indeed and unworthy of the regard lavished on it if it
could prompt only a return to art forms of past centuries. I
have been struck when looking at carvings and sculpture by
such artists as Whalen, Gwynneth Holt and Norman J.
Forrest by a feeling of approach which is strongly reminiscent
of the Celtic artist's approach. There is the same odd,
detached pleasure in the material, in purely aesthetic effect, in
symbolism.

If the Celtic impulse behind the younger sculptors is a
matter for speculation, it is clearly the inspiration of Scottish
painting in the past fifty years. The greatest of the Scottish

painters has been William M'Taggart (1835–1910), who did for
Scotland what Claude Monet did for Europe, and perhaps did
it better. He captured the magic of light actually before the
Impressionists did, and his mastery of it equals the mastery
of the greatest of the Frenchmen. In his later period he sacrificed design, story-content, everything to the transference to
his canvas or paper of his vivid sense-impressions of some
wide sweep of sea and sky. To come upon a M'Taggart in a
sombre city gallery is to emerge from a cave into daylight with
that shock to the retina which causes even the solidest objects
to seem made of blinding light, and the sympathetic vibrations
with which all one's senses respond to this bewitchery of one
of them salute one of the most remarkable achievements in
modern painting. M'Taggart was born near Machrihanish,
in a Gaelic-speaking house. His every brush-stroke quivers
with the Celt's pleasure in brightness—and, for that matter,
with the Celt's close communion with Nature. Those deeper
things, not efforts to construct a 'Celtic Revival' out of motifs
and legends resurrected from a dead past, prove that the
Celtic genius is not done with. In England, there has been no
M'Taggart. And the leading French Impressionists again
were men with a Celtic strain in them. The same passion
for light and movement, with an added delight in jewelled
colour, appears in the watercolours of Arthur Melville (1855–
1904). His keen sensitivity to atmosphere gave him the power
to record with a few bold washes the life of Moorish streets
as M'Taggart recorded his own shores, although Melville's
genius is slighter. An especially remarkable resurgence of the
national trends in art took place in Glasgow in the '80s and
'90s. Slumps had cast no shadows before, and for generations
Glasgow had been an aggressively independent city, a focus
for trade and enterprise, emancipated from the provincial
status by affluence and influence as Venice and Bruges had
once emancipated themselves. Her original merchant princes
had no culture; but she had one or two dealers who were
critics of the first order. They recognized the quality of the
young 'Glasgow School', and encouraged it not only by
marketing its work to rich patrons but by bringing Dutch
and French masterpieces to the city. So the group which had
begun in the studio of W. Y. Macgregor (1855–1923) developed
a European reputation. They turned their backs contemptu-

ously on subject and made aesthetic effect the chief end of their
painting. Great variety of treatment marked the work of the
score or more of painters at one time or another associated
with the Glasgow School, but it differed from M'Taggart's
work in the strong sense of design or pattern, if it shared his
joy in colour and in vigorous, bold treatment. It shared too
his joy in light, and again and again the sunshiny effect of
entering a Glasgow gallery has been noted at a time when
galleries elsewhere were still characterized by a decorous gloom.
The intuitive understanding of Nature was too intense to
permit the Pre-Raphaelite foolishness of leaf-by-leaf study:
most paintings were powerfully subjective interpretations and
earned their 'perpetrators' the usual ridicule. The feeling for
design, and especially for spacing and colour in the design,
owed something to Japanese influence, in the first place
through Whistler, and more directly by the visit paid by E. A.
Hornel and George Henry to Japan itself, which produced a
conception of the picture as a decorative panel in the Oriental
manner. Where the Glasgow School failed, contrasted with
the lone M'Taggart in Edinburgh, was that in championing
aesthetic values they seem to have been strangers to the
dynamic impulses which alone can produce great art.

Such impulse can be glimpsed in one or two of their successors. Colour is the impulse—the national exultation in colour.
In the work of the Glasgow School there is much beauty, but
not a dynamic conviction, nothing to move very deeply or
greatly exalt or excite, whereas the colourists of the present
century here and there emphatically show glimpses of such
power. The master amongst them is, of course, S. J. Peploe
(1871–1935). Where M'Taggart's glory in his subject becomes
infectious through his brush, Peploe's glory in sheer paint
itself enters into any one looking at his canvases, bringing to
the lips even of the least initiated a probably quite unconscious
smile of glee at the superb achievement in every brush-stroke
and at the challenge in the colour. He found inspiration
chiefly in flower pieces and on the shores of Iona. Detail and
colour tones he simplified brilliantly: the paint seems to have
been squeezed from tube to palette and transferred direct and
unsullied to the canvas with an unerring ease. Less powerful
and less unerring, but as bold in his use of colour, is Leslie
Hunter (1879–1936). He could paint Loch Lomondside

X. DESIGN AND ART

1. GLASGOW SCHOOL OF ART: CHARLES RENNIE MACKINTOSH (*Alan Reiach*)

2. NEW SCHOOL, EDINBURGH (*The Scotsman*)

3. ST. ANDREW IN CAEN STONE, ST. MARGARET'S CHURCH, DUNFERMLINE (*Hew Lorimer, Sculptor*)

4. SILVER COMMUNION CUP, MONIFIETH, *c.* 1640 (*Royal Scottish Museum*)

largely with vermilion, viridian, and emerald green and discovered that a Fife village street demanded a more daring palette than the Côte d'Azur. He caught and held some of those moments of fleeting, transcendentally lovely light which occur perhaps only in Scotland and in Norway. Only in the inequality of his work is he a lesser man than Peploe. The followers of the two are many. F. C. B. Cadell (1883–1937) painted in the Peploe tradition, which is still apparent in the work of W. G. Gillies and J. Maclauchlan Milne, who has attached himself to Arran as Peploe and Cadell did to Iona. To-day, as at most times, Scottish painting shows the Celt's preference for Nature above all other themes, and in William M'Taggart, grandson of the great landscape painter, we have another landscapist who is in the first class. He is one of the most distinctively Scottish of the younger painters north of the Border.

The source of the gaiety which has more and more welled up in Scottish art in the last sixty or seventy years should be clear to any one with a knowledge of the pure Celtic strain—the Gael. Among translators of the Gaelic there would appear to have been a conspiracy to select only songs conforming with the melancholic conception of the Celt which arose about the 'fifties of last century. 'Fiona Macleod' was an artist, but any one wishing to know the Gael should be warned against him. It should not be forgotten that George Bernard Shaw is every bit as much a Celt as W. B. Yeats, and that Gaelic song is full of infectious gaiety, as listeners to the waulking songs will appreciate. Moreover, the Gaelic poets are much less interested in any plot or moral content than they are in capturing in the music of their verse the glistening of a pool in the sun or the precise tone of some peak bathed in the evening light, and they do this with a daring and delight reflected perfectly in the paint of M'Taggart or Peploe. Another and a more obvious example of the Celt's preoccupation with colour is the tartan, as I stated earlier. The art of dyeing wool is, astonishing as it may seem, almost exclusively a Celtic one, and the Norse islands of the Orkneys and Shetlands even to-day leave their wools in their natural colours; and again, the preference in the wool-country of the Borders is for the natural wool. But the Celt's passion for colour seems to have been unbroken since the time of the

Druids. While the tartan has the two practical if antithetical uses of identification and camouflage, immense study by an unknown number of generations of weavers has gone to evolving patterns of the highest aesthetic merit, handed on through the years by means of the warping-stick. The constant impulse is to make the colours as brilliant as may be. For war or the chase it was obviously impossible to introduce colours of a tone which would mark out the wearer at once to enemy or quarry; but the 'hunting' tartan has its 'dress' counterpart for ceremonial occasions, and in the dress tartan scarlet will be substituted for brown where it occurs in the hunting version or, where this would have little effect, as in the case of the Stewart, another tartan largely based on scarlet takes the place of the more drab hunting tartan. For those who doubt the Celtic inspiration of the Scottish colourists, I recommend the setting of a Peploe still-life beside a Chisholm tartan or Hunter's *Mill Dam* or *Miss Gibson Jarvie* beside the Macnab or the Grant.

In literature, the Celtic genius still seems to hanker uneasily after the licence of verse. The Gael has come near to writing great novels, supremely great novels, but it is questionable whether he has yet achieved one. Among his novelists the most celebrated to-day is Neil Gunn, the extent of whose powers is still difficult to assess. From the first he has broken through into places where the ordinary story-teller does not stray, and from the first he left us wondering whether he would succeed in gathering transcendent wisdom there or just handfuls of beautiful imaginings. He revealed a power to recapture scents and sounds of an acute significance which might be put to a tremendous use, and yet again he would be content to use the old stock figures of lairds and lads o' pairts to make a conventional Highland novel. But in *The Green Isle of the Great Deep* (1944) he has produced a superb story. This thin volume will slip into a place on a shelf near the top, not only in English but in Gaelic literature. Here at last Tir nan Og is not twilit, but sparkles, bee-drowsed in the noon sun. But the twilight was upon Neil Munro, who preceded Gunn. That there was a vein of genius in Neil Munro there is no denying, but it shone with the provoking Celtic gleam that leads us nowhere by the romantic road of escape, like Paruig Dall in *The Lost Pibroch*. To call Munro a realist because he wrote of disillusionment, as some do, is to accept the 'Fiona Macleod' assessment of the Gael which it is so essential to overturn; but he was a skilful weaver of those romantic yarns which have been one of Scotland's outstanding contributions to literature, from Scott and Stevenson to John Buchan. And the Lowland blood in him came out in the Para Handy stories, which are perhaps his best. To revert to the present, a novelist little known outside Scotland is 'Fionn Mac Colla'. Mac Colla (T. Douglas MacDonald) is not a Gael but a Fifer who has adopted the Gaelic, yet he has earned the remark that 'in a very profound sense his English is the finest Gaelic we have'. Some of the descriptions in his novel *The Albannach*—one of the most distinguished pieces of fiction to come out of the north in a generation—are stanzas of pure Gaelic verse, sensitive to the minutest glimpse of loveliness, such as the transmuting power of a tear-drop. Always, inspiration tends verse-wards. But nearly always it is nostalgic. One or two of the younger poets writing in Gaelic appear to be less twilight-minded: 'Hugh MacDiarmid' gives in translation in the essay which he contributes to *The New Scotland* some remarkable fragments from an epic poem, *The Cuillin*, by Somhairle Mac Gill' Eathain. But not unnaturally there is bitterness and political polemic in them. To find the Gaelic genius pure and unspoiled, it would seem we have still to go back to the eighteenth century and Duncan Ban Macintyre with his childlike delights, whether in his mountains or in his 'Mairi ban og'.

To the Gael, the spoken word has meant more than the written. Not that Gaelic poetry depended on the memories of bards and sennachies, for it was carefully recorded; but its popularity—and indeed all the vigour of Gaelic culture—has been maintained by means of the *ceilidh*, the gathering round the peat-fire in neighbours' houses at which every one is expected to contribute some piece of entertainment, while the women spin or knit. There are stories, songs, music. There are battles of wit, and discussions in which is attained a power of language to be envied by any orator in the south, where vocabularies have sunk to a few hundred overworked words. There is no better illustration of this than the evidence of the crofters as recorded by the Crofters Commission. The *ceilidh* is a precious revival of recreation in its true meaning, a meaning already so nearly forgotten in the Anglo-Saxon world. It was seriously endangered by the strict sabbatarianism of the mid-nineteenth century—not, be it noted, by the penetration of the Reformation to the Highlands—but it is returning to vigorous life. Partly the revival is due to the passing of the evangelical minister, and partly to the work of An Comunn Gaidhealach, the Gaelic Society. In some of the Outer Isles it never lapsed. The *ceilidh* is essentially a social gathering of a high cultural level, but quite informal. The great annual competitive festival of the Gael, equivalent of the Welsh Eisteddfod, is the Mod, held successively in the larger Highland towns and occasionally in Glasgow. The standard of performance on these occasions is remarkable. The finer points of Gaelic music, song, dance, and speech are jealously guarded, and every true Gael is a critic of these things. Highland dancing is probably fallen far below the old standards, but even so it is not to be judged by the decorous performances at Highland balls, still less by what the kilted and be-medalled little girls do at the Highland Games organized as tourist attractions—the last is a mockery of the fiery, abandoned exhibitions once proper to the strongest and bravest clansmen, to indulge the pride and demonstrate their might of muscle and nimbleness of foot. Music, on the other hand, is still the supreme art of the Gael, and no people has a greater national heritage of folk-song. Let me say at once that *Songs of the Hebrides* are not part of it, any more than Macpherson's *Ossian* or the volumes of 'Fiona Macleod' are part of Gaelic literature. It is the old story of romanticizing the Celt again. As C. M. Grieve points out in his *Contemporary Scottish Studies* the romantic title of *Kishmul's Galley* should, in strict accuracy, have been rendered simply as *MacNeill's Boat*. This does not mean that Mrs. Kennedy Fraser's work was not in itself excellent, as indeed *Ossian* is excellent, but only that it is an Anglo-Saxon and not a Celtic conception, and that the work of recording the folk-song of the Gael is not yet begun. The poetic and musical idiom of the Gael cannot be transposed. It has been said that the finest of Italian-trained singers could never achieve with a Gaelic song what the ordinary crofter can achieve. Translation of the words alone destroys nine-tenths of the beauty of the music, because the Gaelic language itself has a beauty which is untranslatable. Its poetry is not a matter of rhyme but of vowel stress. The 'sweet melancholy' of the translations likewise is misleading, and due to the sentimental preferences of the Anglo-Saxon when in musical mood. Here I am forcibly reminded of a photographer who came north to take pictures of Scotland and insisted on taking only what editors 'would clearly recognize at once as Scotch', so perpetuating all the old romantic falsities. This thraldom has done more than anything to curb the growth of musical genius in Scotland. The rich heritage of folk-song has been put to false uses because the Scot, with his economic dependence on the south, has long grown accustomed to looking on his heritage with the eye of the southerner, and genius where it has emerged must have stultified and died for want of any but alien material with which to nourish its powers. The unfulfilment of the promise shown by Hamish MacCunn (1868–1916) is no doubt explained by this. His themes were Scottish; there was no medium to his hand but the medium of the European schools. Francis George Scott alone of Scots composers seems to have realized the predicament and, setting himself to surmount it, found his way to something vital. . . . Here it should be said that the great folk-music heritage includes the music of the pipes. Outside Gaeldom, it is as little understood as the music of the Chinese, and therefore as easily dismissed. But in its highest form, the pibroch, which has been compared with the sonata for subtlety of theme and execution, it has a vital beauty critically appreciated throughout the north-west.

Nearly all Scottish writers and artists to-day agree that Calvinism was as a plague of locusts to Scottish culture, and some of the younger ones have been consistent enough to join the Roman Catholic Church. It is an astonishing judgement. It is a judgement based almost entirely on opinion—opinion which has accumulated support simply because it has hardly ever been challenged—and it is all against the evidence. The grim and austere qualities of what is known as the 'Calvinistic Scot' are not Calvinist qualities, but qualities inherent in the Lowland Scot. Miss M. P. Ramsay, in her invaluable little book on *Calvin and Art*, traces the frugality and austerity of the Scots back to the picture given by Froissart in 1360 and quotes verses of the reign of David II taunting England with the finery which makes her 'thryftless'. She quotes also at length the speech in which Bishop Henry Wardlaw denounces English habits of soft living for their demoralization of the Scots, as a result of which the Parliament of 1430 passed a law against the wearing of rich clothes. The simple explanation of the so-called 'Calvinist' qualities of the Lowland Scot are that, from the thirteenth to the seventeenth century, his ancestors were engaged in a deadly struggle with a much larger and richer neighbour. England could wage the war and leave an ample margin of her wealth and energies for trade; Scotland had to throw everything she had into the fight. And it gave the Lowland Scots the character inevitable in any race which, every few years throughout the centuries, has to make scorched earth of its farmsteads and towns and take to the woods and the hills as guerrillas. It has given them all the grim defects so mercilessly recorded by George Douglas Brown in his *The House with the Green Shutters*, together with indefatigable fighting qualities and a determination to make good the time lost and win prosperity, each for himself. But they have no ancient culture to inherit. A few blackened abbeys were all that the wars left them. The Reformation found a country in which the poor were poverty-stricken: the little wealth was concentrated about the Court and the Church, which imported their culture as they imported their luxuries.

That a form of religion may suppress and wither the artistic impulse of an entire people is a contention without any basis in history. The ban on representational art in Islam merely directed the aesthetic impulses of the Moslem world into channels on which no ban had been placed and ultimately produced an art of special distinction. Rome, which had exercised close supervision of art, provided the inspiration for one of the greatest of all epochs. By the sixteenth century, however, the lowering of the aesthetic standards of ecclesiastical art were paralleled only by the Indulgences and other abuses against which the leaders of the Reformation revolted, and church interiors had become florid and sickly with an unhealthy growth of ornament offending against every canon of aesthetics. A study of Calvin's *Institutes of the Christian Religion* reveals the reformer as a major influence for good upon Christian art. He shrewdly identified aesthetic with moral abuse and laid

down in resounding passages the never-to-be-forgotten
principle that an artist who submits himself to no discipline
is an artist lost.

'But for as much as carving and painting are the gifts of
God', he writes, 'I require that they be both pure and law-
fully used. Lest these things which God has given us for
His glory and for our own benefit be not only defiled by
disorderly abuse, but also turned to our own destruction.'

Not only did he condemn what offended in the churches of
the Roman faith. As Miss Ramsay points out, he warned the
new men of the Renaissance against the danger of mere
sensuality, while exulting with them in the beauty of Creation.

'They see that exquisite workmanship in all their members, from their mouth and their eyes, even to the nails of
their toes, and yet here also they put nature in place of God.'

Is this the vandal of an evil genius who brought a 'blight
upon Scotland'? Even his *Institutes* are exquisite literature.
In the Low Countries, where his influence was most intense,
a great art of the people and of landscape grew up. In France,
the Huguenots were master-craftsmen whose exile enriched
countries from England to South Africa. In Scotland, there
was neither a tradition of craftsmanship, wealth to encourage
it, nor media to provoke experiment. There was little wood,
metals were brought only at a great cost from England or
Sweden, and a country whose principal exports included fish
and pole-cat skins would not be exchanging those things for
pigments or marble in the markets of Flanders. The Reformation had little immediate cultural effect, unless the end of the
flow of wealth to Rome produced any increase in patronage.
The one outstanding piece of destruction of the country's
cultural heritage was the ruining of St. Andrews Cathedral by
the mob, although Knox had just preached in it a sermon
against the defiling of the temple. Certainly, pictures and
ornaments were removed, in accordance with Calvin's teaching.
Much of the plate was taken by the fleeing priests themselves:
that from Glasgow Cathedral went to the Scots College in
Paris. No doubt most of this plate was elaborate silver-gilt
work from Augsburg or Nuremberg, and the Queen Mary
Cup of St. John's Church at Perth is one of the few remaining
examples. By the end of the sixteenth century this interesting

but overwrought silver had begun to be replaced by chaste communion cups of exquisite proportion and grace which number among them—in the kirks of Forgue, Dalry, Currie, Monifieth, for example—some of the most perfect examples of silver craftsmanship in existence. At last Scotland was producing craftsmen. Their work had the same bracing functional severity and pleasure in the sheer qualities of the material which characterizes much other work done under Calvinist influence. Examples may be seen in Puritan furniture and silverwork in England. Many of the kirks erected by the Reformers show the same pleasing simplicity and cleanness of line—Reay and Dunnett, both in Caithness, are illustrated by Hurd and Reiach in their most useful little book, *Building Scotland*. The town of Inveraray shows the domestic aspect of the same tendency. Indeed, before the death of John Knox Scotland had for the first time in four centuries begun to build up the margin of supply over demand, the prosperity which is a necessary condition of cultural development. The pruning of meaningless efflorescence—that dissipator and diverter of creative energies—effected by Calvinism in Europe had no opportunity in Scotland; but its strict influence had no bad effect on the roots of the arts, which grew in strength. Soon in the most strongly Calvinist parts of Scotland—the south and the south-west—great new craft-industries were growing up, similar to the industries which grew up wherever Huguenot exiles settled. The woollen industry and the weavers and lace-workers of Ayrshire parallel the Spitalfields weavers in London, who fled France after the Revocation of the Edict of Nantes. Indeed, a profound and logical sense of functional design is a quality widely found in the industrial Lowlands. It is linked with the gift for engineering. No doubt it explains why the *Queen Mary*, seen beside the *Normandie* or, even more markedly, beside such ships as the *Bremen* or the *Conte di Savoia*, has the effect of a Savile Row suit contrasted with the supreme effort of a multiple tailor. Too often, this link between Puritanism and functionalism is overlooked by art critics and historians.

The Celt's love of Nature and its influence on Scottish art has been remarked on. It is a pagan urge, a primeval or child-like wonder or joy in natural phenomena. Calvinism gave moral sanction to it. Calvin looked on all beauty, whether of the hills and fields or of the human body, as the manifestation of God. Not until the Reformation was Europe freed from man's preoccupation with man in art, and the first great school of land and seascape, from Wouvermans and Cuyp to Ruisdael and Hobbema, arose in the Calvinist Low Countries. In Scotland there seems to have been no native painter at all until Jamesone began to practise early in the seventeenth century, but the new feeling for Nature had already appeared in poetry. Alexander Hume, minister of Logie, and others including later the Covenanting preachers themselves drew spiritual strength from the earth about them, especially perhaps from the grandeur of hill and storm. Miss Ramsay strikes a shrewd comparison between the old weaver, Jamie Stewart, who used to leave his loom and go out bareheaded into the thunderstorm, saying, 'It's my Father's voice and I like well to hear it', and a great passage in the *Institutes*:

> 'How great a strength it is . . . with His only beck, some-
> times to shake the heaven with noise of thunders . . . and
> by and by the same God when He lists in one moment to
> make fair weather.'

The parallel with the Dutch school of landscape painting came only with the eighteenth century. It emerged, appropriately, with a minister of the Kirk, John Thomson of Duddingston (1778–1840), but he rejected the example of the Dutch School for that of Claude and Poussin, whose treatment matched his urge to put the wild mountains and coasts of his own country on canvas. Of all the Scottish School, he approaches most nearly to Turner, whose friend he was. Not content with pure representation, which Girtin and other landscapists in the south were revelling in, he strove always for something more transcendental. He had, in fact, Calvin's attitude to Nature. He was an amateur, his work unequal; but none of his successors in the prolific Scottish school of landscape ever quite achieved what he achieved in, for example, *Castle Baan*.

Literature is the one field of culture in which the 'Calvinist' —the Lowland—element did not have to begin from the beginning. There were not many men of the intellectual stature of Buchanan among the Reformers, but they num-bered many of the keenest minds in the old church, and

intellectual activity remained high until the crushing of the
Huguenots severed the link between France and Scotland.
Even the native bigotry and tyrannies of the seventeenth
century could not suppress the development of the ballad,
equivalent of the song-making of the Celt. This was the
background from which Sir Walter Scott emerged. But the
arrival of a literature sprung directly from the grim but fierce
genius lurking in the Lowland Scot had to wait until later in
the nineteenth century. When it came, there was nothing
gracious or captivating in it; defiant and explosive, it made all
other writing of the time seem slight. In Thomas Carlyle
all the straining power and enterprise and determination which
rendered the great ships and machines of the Clyde supreme
took intellectual form and made this man of Calvinist Scots
stock supreme in the world of letters. His mind ranged up
and down the universe and had scant time for his own country
or people. This grim, ruthless, explosive vein of genius seemed
to die with him. R. L. Stevenson touched upon it in his great,
unfinished *Weir of Hermiston*. Then it appeared again. The
sentimental stories of 'Ian Maclaren' and the 'kailyard school'
of novelists, selling to the world a saccharine conception of the
Scot all the more damaging because of the half-truths of it,
provoked a fierce reaction among one or two able writers.
They went to the opposite extreme. The two ablest have died
with great things in them still unwritten. The first of them
was George Douglas Brown (1869–1902), who, in his *The House
with the Green Shutters*, deliberately suppressed the gentler
longings and the beauty of life in the setting down of which
he had a rare mastery—suppressed them to lay on the lash
where he knew it was needed. His one book is a bitter-
sounding, sombre masterpiece. Had its end been more subtle,
it would have been one of the greatest novels in the language,
but none of the crop of imitations of it between the two wars
in any way approaches it. The other great scourger of the
sentimental is Lewis Grassic Gibbon, whose masterpiece is
his trilogy of novels, *Sunset Song*, *Cloud Howe* and *Grey
Granite*. They are written in the dialect of the Mearns, in a
subtle rhythm which makes each a prose poem and, like George
Douglas Brown's book, they deal with one small town. Like
Brown, Gibbon is a master of sensitive description and yet
his work quivers with power like some mighty engine. There

I

appeared to be an echo of this in Dr. Cronin's *Hatter's Castle*, but the echo seems to have died away on the exotic shores of *Grand Canary*. John Barke is another novelist who has built some impressive writing out of Lowland materials. But the nature of the Lowland mind makes it an easy prey to psychological clap-trap and sex, so that there has been a tendency in the past ten years for writers—even quite promising writers —to turn with relish to a bogus-Freudian rooting and snuffling for nameless tit-bits in the middens of their subconscious. Poetry, on the other hand, can show a tale of mounting achievement. It has been emancipated after nearly a century of humiliating sentimentality, and 'couthieness' and aimless construction. No writer has done so much to re-establish it as C. M. Grieve—'Hugh MacDiarmid'—who gave it an intellectual content which had been conspicuously absent, and who is now the foremost lyric poet in Scotland. Latterly he has given his verse a greater and greater burden to bear—has made it the vehicle of polemic and satire which, right and justifiable though they may be, have crippled the simple grace of the lyrics of his *Sangschaw* and *Penny Wheep*, which appeared in 1925 and 1926. He has been criticized for not using prose for the theme of such a piece as *To Circumjack Cencrastus*. But he is one of the most vital and powerful poets of to-day, a merciless enemy of all that is false and a tireless champion of what is genuine in Scottish culture. He has solved the problem of which of the many Scots dialects to choose for medium by inventing a synthetic Scots in which numerous alien words or scientific terms float easily as required. This dialect difficulty has not prevented a great revival of vernacular verse, some of which is in the front rank judged by any standard: Mrs. Violet Jacob's *Howe of the Mearns*, for example, Marion Angus's *The Turn o' the Day*, and many poems by Charles Murray, William Soutar and Lewis Spence, who reverts to Middle Scots, the Scots of four centuries ago, for his medium. It is interesting, and surely significant, how wholeheartedly the younger poets have adopted the vernacular and made it live as it has not lived since the day of Burns. Indeed, in the past twenty years, few Scots poets of distinction have adopted English as their principal medium; of these Edwin Muir is one of the most outstanding.

This question of the vernacular is of considerable importance for the development of a truly national culture in Scotland.
North of the Tweed there are three language groups: Gaelic,
English, and the vernacular dialects. Each represents a viewpoint. Gaelic was once the tongue of all Scotland. Now it is
spoken by rather more than 100,000 people out of five millions,
and of that minority nearly all are bilingual; so that Gaelic
is mainly a vehicle of domestic intercourse, and that in a
more and more narrow sense as the years go by. English is
the standard language, the language of advancement, understood by all. For more than two centuries it has been the
accepted medium of the bulk of Scots writers, and the vernacular trend of the poets is probably looked on by most
middle-class Scots as eccentricity. Yet English is the *natural*
tongue of a minority perhaps not greatly exceeding the Gaelic
minority. Most Scots can speak a grammatical enough
English when they choose, but their ordinary conversation is
full of vernacular words, and many of their most expressive
phrases are based on local dialect. Scots in itself is not a mere
dialect of English, like Cockney or Somerset, but another
tongue, with a history and literature of its own and independent
bonds with French and other languages. In common usage
it has deteriorated and become vulgarized by neglect, but its
roots are in the Age of the Makars—the age of the sixteenth
century Scots Chaucerians, Dunbar and Henryson. Here again
John Knox has been the target of modern critics, this time for
making English his vehicle and for discrediting the poetry
of the makars by damning it as popish and so reducing Scots
to a peasant dialect; but the fact remains that Allan Ramsay,
two centuries later, and the titled ladies who composed the
'Auld Scots Sangs' still wrote and spoke in the so-called
'peasant dialect'. Certainly, it had been much anglicized.
But for a cause of the spread of English there is no need to
look further than the political and economic implications of
the Union. Inevitably, an Anglo-Scottish top-layer formed
upon Scots society, and the rift between was a rift not only
of language but of outlook. The tree of Scots culture will
never grow as great as it might until all its roots can strike
across this rift and find nourishment in the substratum.
Recognizing this, C. M. Grieve has demanded a return to the
vernacular. He claims that only through this medium can

the real feelings of the Scots people to-day be got at, and that tremendous new forces will flow into Scots culture as a result. He maintains, further, that this end is being deliberately thwarted by English and Anglo-Scots who realize that the new force would 'burst the existing system in Scotland into smithereens'. His opponents say the vernacular has lapsed too far to be revived. This is a reasonable criticism of the attempts to go back to Dunbar: as well might English poets go back to Chaucer—the best medium is the means of expression through which a poet's thought is most readily understood by his contemporaries. But the vernacular of the ordinary Scots family, especially the family uncontaminated by the vulgarisms of city slang, is powerful, lively and colourful, and the Scot, even if he has never used it and only known it as a background, turns to it with a strange excitement. Time and again it fits his thought like a glove. Grieve maintains the objection to its use is a class objection—that it is the language of the workers. But I think the true objection is that every writer instinctively writes for the widest possible public, which demands the use of English.

It is in the amenities and in the popular aspect of culture that Scotland has most leeway to make up. Some excellent achievements mark the years preceding the outbreak of war, but most of them remained beacons in a wilderness which had lasted for a century during which no people possessing a lovely country had done less to preserve and enhance its loveliness. In other small European countries the 'twenties and 'thirties saw an eager awakening of pride and purpose, despite poverty and unrest, and culture could claim a place in the forefront of the advance to prosperity and well-being. The new architecture of Sweden and Holland, Switzerland, and Czechoslovakia, initiative in industrial design such as Orrefors glass, Skånsen and the Danish nurture of folk-culture —in a few years those things won from the world a respect and admiration which had nothing to do with commerce or politics. Those countries had not cultural traditions greater than Scotland's. Their degree of wealth was comparable to Scotland's. Why, it was asked, did Scotland lag? The answer seems to lie in the ugly, sloughed skin of nineteenth-century industrial provincialism when the only values were money values and the only unit that mattered was the individual. In that time cultural values went the way of ethical ones.

This utter insensitiveness to aesthetic impulses found its nadir in housing design between the two wars. The speculative builder, bereft of the vestiges of a craftsman's conscience which rendered the old tenements at least solid, was permitted to surround even Edinburgh itself with mass-produced bungalows and flatted villas as unfitted for the climate as they are foreign to the landscape. Certain features are functionally proper to Scots domestic architecture: a simple, four-square exterior, because stone is the national building material, prominent chimneys and modest windows, because of the need to conserve warmth. The housing schemes of the 'thirties gave heed neither to the wisdom of the past nor to progressive thought. Most of them had not even the English housing estate's pathetic, flimsy concessions to amenity, flattering the possible purchaser by the assumption that he still possessed some sort of taste. They were stark commercialism. They insulted by their existence not only the cities, but some of the loveliest of the Highland straths. Not even the traditional coat of whitewash relieved the drab harl of them. But the very uncompromising crudity of them was a blessing, for by the mid-'thirties they had wakened a substantial body of criticism which is certainly going to bear fruit in post-war building plans. A vigorous stand has been made by the younger architects. Men who might easily have nurtured a precious regard for exotic trends were provoked to a healthy loyalty to traditional virtues, which they easily reconciled with contemporary developments, and the encouragement given by the Saltire Society to pride in past achievement has greatly aided this welding of old and new. Fruits of continuity can be seen in a number of undertakings, good examples of which are the Falkirk and Fife miners' housing schemes illustrated by Reiach and Hurd in *Building Scotland*. Many new private houses too have adapted the old tradition of plain, whitewashed walls with painted surrounds to the windows and roofs of blue slate or red pantiles, to the benefit of some corners at least of the Scottish landscape. The functionalism of Charles Rennie Mackintosh (1868–1928) was a logical development of the simplicity of the traditional style, although the Glasgow School of Art (1894) remained his solitary work in his own country throughout a generation when his influence was spreading across the Continent. Now the lesson he taught seems to be coming home. The Glasgow Empire Exhibition had, like all great exhibitions, a rather unbalancing effect, on the one hand giving scope to some of the best of the new architects such as Thomas Tait and Basil Spence, on the other inducing a certain over-emphasis of 'exhibitionist' features, very marked in one great public building at least. But some of the newer schools are admirable—comparable with anything abroad; and the same can be said of a select few industrial structures, such as the buildings at the Comrie coal-pit in Fife. Public bodies have indeed been showing a degree of enlightment which may yet compensate us for the dreadful heritage of 'baronial' libraries and town halls which they built three or four generations ago. But there is still an immense task to educate the mass of the Scottish people to repudiate the formless, colourless existence which they have led for a hundred years.

This grey existence is another thing which has been flung in the teeth of Presbyterianism, when the real cause is the lapse into provincialism. Since 1707 Scotland has tended to import the English culture and manner of life instead of nourishing her own, to the impoverishment not only of herself but of the kingdom as a whole. To the visitor, this is less noticeable by day. He pays due homage to the medieval skyline and the faultless neo-classicism of Edinburgh and sees with awe the clangour of the Vulcan's forge of Glasgow, but at the end of the day he searches vainly for the intimate, quickening, cultural essence of the people. Unless he has a rare knowledge of where to search, he finds nothing that can be called a Scottish art of living. For example, if he is the right sort of visitor, he looks for the food and drink of the country. He will not find it in any public eating-place in the cities, and few places in the country can provide it. Scots food has come to be regarded by hotel-keepers much as the vernacular is regarded by polite society—as a vulgar, if occasionally amusing anachronism. The costly Tay salmon will in season find a place on the menu; but the humble herring, more delicious, more nourishing, and a staple article in the old Scots diet, is neither appreciated nor understood by the foreign *chefs* who rule the restaurants. The broth of the country is never among the *plats du jour*. The uses of the other great staple of the Scots diet, oatmeal, are almost forgotten: the making of porridge is an art lost to all but a few, and the oat itself has been 'pre-digested' by numerous commercial processes which sadden those who know the nutty flavour and sublime, ineffable texture which define porridge as it once was eaten. These are not small matters. The food of Sweden or of Austria, of Holland or of Russia connotes a particular quality of conviviality, of fellowship, for the stranger an intimate sharing in another mode of life. Food has always been the token of hospitality: to deny one's birthright for a mess of imported pottage can only be the symbol of a much profounder falsifica-tion. The pride of the *patisseries* of Paris is paralleled in Scotland not by the celebrated tea-shops of Edinburgh and Glasgow, but by a few cottars and crofters who still—for a few pence—delight in providing the stranger with scones hot from the girdle, thick oatcakes, fresh butter and a brew of tea. . . . In the cities, the visitor will likewise be disappointed when he looks for entertainment. He will be eager to discover what this country of passionate history and mighty conceptions of industry has distilled into its drama; but the theatres will offer him nothing but an English touring company or two. Such, at least, was the case until the present war. But the war has happily spurred on the revolt against provincialism. No national theatre, nor anything approaching it, has emerged as yet, but the demand for it grows. Glasgow has taken the lead by forming a Citizen's Theatre, and there are far-reaching hopes not only that it may eventually be subsidized by the City but that it will be linked with an all-embracing scheme for the encouragement of the arts in general. Over a period of years there has been a growing interest in the stage which has reached out even into the villages through the medium of the Drama Festivals. The standard of acting and of pro-duction is remarkably high, although no fundamentally Scottish drama has emerged as yet. It is perhaps only when one contemplates the attempt of a small country to recover its cultural vigour that the dangers latent in 'canned' entertain-ment such as the commercial cinema and the radio are seen in full perspective. So far, in the theatre, the only real challenge issued from Scotland which is effective against the ruthless competition has been that of the vernacular comedian, and he is rarely a success out of his own country. To find him at his best, he should be looked for in the Glasgow pantomimes.

Far more than any religious prejudices, the Scottish educational tradition has been inimical to the free development of a national culture. Things are changing now, but it will be a hard task to eradicate the tyranny of the 'three R's'—a tyranny which served its purpose by making the Scots a grimly efficient and mentally disciplined phalanx of a race, capable of cutting their way through to success against almost any odds. 'It is, however,' wrote Sir Alexander MacEwen in 1932, 'open to doubt whether under our present system the average primary or even secondary school child carries away with him anything which may be described as of permanent intellectual value. It is, unfortunately, possible to take a University degree and yet be devoid of the civilizing influence of literature, art, and music as a new born babe.' This old academic bias is going. But there is a new danger, to which perhaps the Scot is peculiarly subject, that education may tend to become a vocational preparation instead of a preparation for life. Through many centuries the conviction has been forced on the Scot that work is in itself a virtue and an end; and, while this is by no means the curse which some of the younger writers make it out to be, it must be balanced by an equal appreciation of the virtue of leisure. There is a growing awareness, however, that if the Scot is to hold his head up among the civilized peoples he must be given his proper cultural background—that his life will be a richer, fuller thing if he learns at his mother's knee not English nursery rhymes but fragments of his own natural heritage in such things, from the lovely fairy lore of the Gael through the vernacular songs to the incomparable children's verses of R. L. Stevenson, and if for his grounding in great literature he is directed first not across the Border to Shakespeare and Milton but to the Celtic bards and to the makars. Until this comes about, he will remain intellectually an uneasy half-breed. And here the question of language again enters. The Gaelic is the ancient language of all Scotland, precisely as Welsh belongs to all Wales; but even where it is taught in schools it is taught as a dead language or as a foreign tongue, not as the natural medium. Thus 'Hugh MacDiarmid', quoting from 'Fionn

Mac Colla's ' *Cuis na Canain*. Even by those who must allow for the passionate Celticism of these writers, it must be admitted that it is a cultural enormity to permit a language so lovely and expressive to die. Mac Colla urges not only that Gaelic be 'the medium of instruction in all subjects in every school in the Gaidhealtachd', but also that it be made 'a compulsory second language in every other Scottish school'. There is a strong secondary argument for bilingualism in that it greatly increases the ease with which foreign languages may be learned, more especially as the Gaelic has certain close affinities both with French and with German. The obvious sequel to any broad scheme for restoring the balance of Gaelic language and culture would be the establishment of a Gaelic University, and this too has been mooted by many thinking Scots.

Another essential for the healthy growth of Scottish culture is an informed and wise body of critics. Once—in the day of *The Edinburgh Review*—the stronghold of literary criticism, Scotland has for some reason for a long time shunned art and literary critics. Some of her authors write excellent critical essays from time to time, but probably the only one of them doing this regularly enough to rank among first-rate critics on an international plane is Edwin Muir, and his vehicle is more often than not a London periodical. Of frank yet constructive art criticism there is almost none. It would be untrue to say there are no art critics, as it would be to say there are no literary critics, but the opportunities for them are lacking. William M'Cance's is a name which occurs, but he again, like Muir, has found little or no outlet in his own country. Distinguished work has frequently appeared in *The Modern Scot*, but not until a proper assessment of cultural values is taken seriously by the few more popular periodicals and by the press will the people even begin to realize that all has not been well with Scottish culture.

Nothing has contributed more to the disunity of Scotland than the false cleavage between Highland and Lowland cultures. They are distinct, certainly, but it is the distinction between the elements of the *yang* and *yin* in Chinese metaphysics—complements, without which wholeness cannot be. There can be no equipoise in the Scottish people, no fullness of living, no consummation, until those vital elements are reconciled. Were the two merely severed, fusion would be less difficult. Each, however, has been grotesquely falsified, the Celt by emphasis on his romanticism—his Achilles' heel, the Lowlander by exaggeration of the sentimentality which is his weak point. The aim and end of it all has been the old, old segregation of the Celt, coupled with an attempt to establish the racial oneness of Lowlander and Englishman. Some writers profess to see behind this a diabolical political plot devised for the subjection of Scotland, but who the truly Olympian plotters were has never been disclosed, and it seems more reasonable to attribute what has happened to the simple antagonism between the interests of individuals and the interests of a people. In spite of political engineering, the Scots remained one people until long after the 'Forty-five. Only with the coming of the Industrial Revolution did the Celt come to be looked upon by certain Lowlanders as an inferior to be exploited—Lowlanders who saw also that their interests were closely bound up with England's. It is to those men and their legacy we must attribute ultimately the triumph of the Celtic Twilight and Balmoralism, the 'Kailyaird' writers and the couthie *genre* school of painting, and all the forces which depicted the Highlander as a feckless oddity or the Lowlander as a rustic 'character' with heart of gold. If those travesties of our culture are being overturned, if the true outline and identity of Scotland are at last taking shape through the haar, it must not be looked upon as a break-away from England. Only through discovery of her own identity will Scotland ever contribute her full quota to the partnership with England and to the commonwealth of nations. She is not an ancient nation, as the romantics would have us believe, but merely a nation with a long, long childhood and adolescence, which perhaps in the end are not bad things.

BOOKS ON SCOTLAND

No short list of books about Scotland can be comprehensive: writers tend to the particular rather than to the general. An idea of the Scots character from books can only be absorbed by wide reading of such works as 'Jupiter' Carlyle's *Autobiography* and Lord Cockburn's *Memorials*. Among recent sketches, A. G. Macdonell's *My Scotland* (1937) is caustic but stimulating. Innes of Learney's *The Tartans, Clans and Families of Scotland* (1938) indicates the pattern of clan organization. On the country and its climate, I still think Prof. Geikie's *The Scenery of Scotland* the most readable work. For a history reference book, Hume Brown's *History of Scotland* (1902) is standard and I should recommend too, Dicey and Rait's *Thoughts on the Union* (1920), while Miss I. F. Grant's *Social and Economic Development of Scotland before 1603* (1930) covers ground otherwise untouched. On the spirit of the Kirk, I know of nothing to beat Dr. Rainy's *Three Lectures on the Church of Scotland* (1883). A. R. G. M'Millan's *Evolution of the Scots Judiciary* (1941) is recommended; and on the same subject, Lord Normand's Presidential Address to the Holdsworth Club of Birmingham (1941). J. Kerr's *Scottish Education: Schools and Universities* (1913) is a standard work. In *How Scotland is Governed* (1938), C. de B. Murray sketches the working of Scottish institutions in general. Dealing with the present state of the country, Dr. Bowie covers a wide field in *The Future of Scotland* (1939), and the Scottish Convention's *Hansard on Scotland* (1942) is invaluable. Prof. J. M. Mackintosh's pamphlet, *The Health of Scotland* (1943), is also excellent. The late Sir Alexander MacEwen's *The Thistle and the Rose* (1932) represents the view of a staunch but not extreme Nationalist. Peter F. Anson's *The Sea Fisheries of Scotland* (1939) puts a huge problem in a nutshell. The Scottish Economic Committee's *Report on the Highlands and Islands of Scotland* (1938) is indispensable; and other useful productions of this Committee are *Light Industries in Scotland* (1938) and *Scotland's Industrial Future* (1939). The *Report on Hydro-Electric Development in Scotland* (1942) is essential. W. M. Ballantine's *Rebuilding a Nation* (1944) presents the housing situation in small compass. And I recommend also James A. A. Porteous's pamphlet, *The Wealth of Scotland*.

There are many books on Scottish philosophy, but for a general picture none is better than Prof. Laurie's *Scottish Thought in its National Development* (1902). Recent contributions to the arts are discussed by C. M. Grieve in *Contemporary Scottish Studies* (1926). The Gaelic background is to be found in Magnus Maclean's *The Literature of the Highlands* (1925), and the Lowlands in T. F. Henderson's *Scottish Vernacular Literature* (1910). Edwin Muir's *Scott and Scotland* (1935) should be read. I have quoted Miss M. P. Ramsay's now out-of-print *Calvin and Art* (1938), and also *Planning Scotland* (1941), by Alan Reiach and Robert Hurd. John Tonge's *The Arts in Scotland* (1938) came out with the Scottish Exhibition at Burlington House. Dr. Honeyman's article on 'Scottish Painting' in *The Studio* for September 1943, is comprehensive and well illustrated. The earlier numbers of *Scottish Woollens* (from 1931), published by the Scottish Woollen Manufacturers' Association, contain invaluable material on the tartans and tweeds. The printing craft is treated of in the Stationery Office publication, *Printing and the Allied Trades in Scotland* (1937). The present writer's articles on 'Scottish Church Plate' and on 'Highland Weapons at the Royal Academy' in *The Connoisseur*, Vol. CIV, No. 456, and Vol. CIII, No. 450 (1939) may be of use.

INDEX

133

PRINTED IN GREAT BRITAIN
BY WESTERN PRINTING SERVICES LTD., BRISTOL.